I0089018

# FIT FOR LIFE

# FIT FOR LIFE

*Think It, Do It, Be It!*

SABA MOOR-DOUCETTE

Copyright ©2018 by Saba Moor-Doucette

All rights reserved. This book or any portion thereof
may not be reproduced or used in any manner whatsoever
without the express written permission of the publisher
except for the use of brief quotations in a book review.

Printed in the United States of America

First Printing, 2018

ISBN-13: 978-1-945949-86-9 print edition
ISBN-13: 978-1-947637-90-0 ebook edition

Disclaimer
The methods described in this book are the author's personal
thoughts. The authors and publisher advise readers to take
full responsibility and to not take risks beyond your level of
experience, aptitude, and comfort level. This book is not intended
as a substitute for the medical advice of a physician, and the
reader should regularly consult a physician in matters relating to
his/her health. Any use of this information is at your own risk.

Book cover design by Flower Perdew

Waterside Press
2055 Oxford Ave
Cardiff, CA 92007
www.waterside.com

# TABLE OF CONTENTS

# INTRODUCTION

## About Saba

When she was sixty-eight years old, Saba saw her best friend lose thirty-five pounds and have the courage to enter a local bikini contest. Inspired by this, she made the decision right then and there to start limiting the effects of aging on her own body and mind as much as possible, and to be fit and youthful for life.

She began with some simple exercises, and quickly started eliminating foods that didn't help her function at the highest energy levels possible. As time went on, Saba began developing her own workouts, creating a healthy and delicious food plan, and incorporating her experience as a spiritual (mind-body) practitioner into her health and fitness routine.

All of this would ultimately translate into an inspired and unique training regimen, leading to a succession of Bikini Diva contest wins. Before she knew it, Saba had a weekly online radio and video program, was creating fitness videos training others of all ages, and igniting her passion for not only reaching her own goals, but for helping others reach theirs.

"I wanted to inspire others the way I was inspired by my friend, and I suddenly realized that my core talents, personality, and passion were coming together in a wonderful and unexpected way. I have a gift for helping others reach their goals, and I absolutely love sharing that gift!"

Health and fitness had suddenly become a way of life for Saba, as she won her first international title at sixty-nine years of age, and at seventy, became a certified personal trainer and began devouring all the health and fitness information she could find.

For the next two years, she competed in Bikini Diva and Sports Model competitions, qualified for Team USA, and ultimately won the Senior Division International Gold Medal in both Bikini Diva and Sports Model competitions.

The excitement of getting that energy and youthful body back after sixty-eight years was so invigorating that she decided to share her experience with her ninety-seven year old mother Dorothy, or "Bubby" as she is lovingly nicknamed. In no time at all, with Saba's guidance, persistence, and compassion, Bubby's mind and body, her whole life really, changed for the better. She had more spring in her step, her mind seemed to be clearer and sharper than in previous years. Most importantly, she was enjoying life again and her sense of humor came roaring back!

Bubby is living an active and healthy life at one hundred and three, and shared Saba's secrets with all of her friends at the senior center and with anyone else who asks her how she stays so fit and alert. They even did a workout video together called "For Seniors and Older."

At this point, it had become clear that Saba's mission in life was to help as many people as possible learn through her combination of diet, exercise, affirmations, and visualizations, that they too can be fit for life. Throughout this book, you will receive tips on how to use these techniques in your everyday life on your way to getting the body you always dreamed you could have. As a side benefit, you might also be equally as pleased with the effect this will have on your mental and emotional states.

You're never too old to start. After all, Saba started at the ripe old age of sixty-eight, and reached every goal she set for herself. With her Think It, Do It, Be It method, she taught herself to change her thinking and change her body.

## About the Book

I wrote this book as a guide for men, women, kids, teens, and anyone who wants to get into shape and have the body and the vibrant health they have always desired. You will learn how to change your thinking to more perfectly harmonize with the vision of your dreams. In this easy to read book, you will develop healthy and effective habits and actions that can be used to achieve personal health and beauty, as well as virtually any goal you desire in life.

The Think It, Do It, Be It method is not hard. The principles are sound, but it does take practice. If you follow the guidance in this book and combine it with an authentic desire to change your current habits and thought patterns concerning your health and fitness, success in reaching your goals is all but guaranteed.

As I developed the Think It, Do It, Be It method, I was noticing that not only was I changing my body, but my whole life was changing along with it. I learned how to build a strong foundation so that every aspect of my life was becoming easier to manage. Now I want to pass on to you the hard-earned information I have learned so that you can experience what it's like to live your life with the Think It, Do It, Be It method. I'll even guide you through a complete day of putting Think It, Do It, Be It into action, so that you can learn all of my secrets and create the kind of life you've always dreamed you could have.

This book will teach you how to make every minute count as you develop new eating and fitness habits, as well as anti-aging techniques that will leave you looking and feeling younger and more vibrant. You will also learn how to fit exercise and diet into your busy day. This method can work for anyone, whether you already have good fitness habits or never seem to have time to go to the gym. You will learn the quickest and best ways to work out anywhere, at home, at work, in the gym, and even in your car. That's right.

With my special *Autosize* workout, you can even turn your car into your own private gym. How great is that?

This book will also help you build a strong foundation with your eating habits and show you an assortment of products that will help you condition your body both inside and out. I also created a nine-day diet I often use when my body needs extra toning and muscle building. I call it "The Weight-Off Muscle-On Diet."

# Why is This Book Different?

Many of you have tried different diets and exercise regimens over the years, only to quickly find yourself slipping back into your old destructive eating and exercise habits. This continuous loop of seesaw dieting never seems to work for any length of time. That is because you tried to "willpower" yourself through the process, probably hating it the whole way. If you don't change how you think about your body and yourself, you will ultimately return to negative thoughts and habits. This book is meant to end that cycle and change your thinking and your life forever.

Our lives are governed by our state of mind. If we want to change anything in our lives, we must start by changing how we think about the thing we are trying to change. We must break our old mental and physical habits and build a foundation of new habits that contribute more positively to our lives. Saba's Fit for Life focuses strongly on transforming both your body and your mind to create a permanent shift in how you view yourself, both inside and out.

I am very excited to be sharing these proven methods for getting into shape, as well as my techniques for keeping your face and body soft and youthful looking, while keeping your mind clear and alert. If you commit to spending time going through the daily routines and following my tips and techniques, you can reach your goal of losing weight, building muscle, living a healthier lifestyle, looking healthier and more youthful, and staying *Fit for Life*.

Thank you to my husband Jeff
for all of his help. I could not have
done this without him.

# CHAPTER 1:
# HOW IT ALL BEGAN

## The *Autosize* Accident

They say there are no accidents. But an "accidental" workout started me on my journey of health, fitness, and anti-aging.

To tell you how *Autosize* started, we have to go back to when I was in my fifties. Like most of you, I live a busy life. I had kids, grandkids, a career, and absolutely no time to fit in a workout at a gym. I had danced since I was a kid, so keeping in shape was a very important priority to me. But how?

At the time, I was writing, producing, and directing while running a production company. I was sitting at a desk for many hours or sitting in my car while driving from Los Angeles to Orange County. When I wasn't doing that, I was helping my daughter by picking up my grandkids, going to their school functions, taking them to after-school programs, and running errands of all kinds. I wasn't getting much exercise, couldn't find the time to go to a gym, and didn't have the energy to work out at home after that long day and that long drive.

1

One day, during my morning meditation, I realized that I hadn't been to a dance class or the gym in a year. Another thing I noticed as I got older was that things on my body started giving in to gravity. My stomach was not as tight as it used to be, my butt was getting softer and starting to droop, and I was developing flab on my arms. But the biggest thing for me was that I found myself getting tired more often, and it was harder to do the things I love doing.

Isn't it funny that when life fills up, the first thing we start to ignore is our body? Just when our body needs more strength, energy, and focus, we turn instead to coffee, sugar, or some other stimulant to get us through the next hour, and then feel even more tired and listless an hour later. That's kind of like buying an expensive car and never putting oil in it or getting it washed or properly serviced. Chances are, that beautiful car isn't going to stay beautiful or perform very well for long.

People have been known to do just about everything in their cars. They eat, sleep, carry on phone conversations, do business, put on makeup, shave, and some people even live in their cars. One day, I decided that instead of being bored while waiting for a light to change, picking up the kids from school, or one of the many other things I wait for in my car, I should do a workout!

That day, as I sat in my car waiting for the kids to come out of school, I was thinking what a waste of time it was just sitting in my car doing nothing. To ease my boredom, I got out of the car, put my hands on the hood, and stretched my back. That felt good. When I got back in the car, I started thinking about my workouts at the gym and how I missed them. I reached for a tissue in a box on the floor on the passenger side and turned it into a stretch. Then my mind went into creative mode. I started thinking, "I wonder how many things I can use in the car to help with a workout?"

Luckily for me, the kids were a little late that day, so I had some time to be creative. I grabbed the steering wheel and squeezed it. I slipped my knees under my steering wheel and lifted my heels to apply more pressure. Wow! To my surprise, it felt just like working out with the equipment at the gym. I started having fun creating new exercises and finding new ways to use my car as a gym.

Over the next couple of weeks, I created a full-body exercise workout that I could do in my car. When the kids asked me, "What are you doing, Grandma?" I would tell them, "I'm working out because I don't have time to go to the gym today." I decided to call my workout, *Autosize.*

I realized early on that for safety reasons it probably wasn't a good idea to do any part of the workout while the car was moving, but every time I hit a red light, stop sign, railroad crossing, or found myself just waiting, I turned it into an opportunity to exercise and stay fit. Maybe it was only a little isometric squeeze or a stretch, but I was doing something and it felt great.

Over the years, I "Autosized" in my car whenever I got the chance. It's just amazing how many minutes of a workout can add up and be beneficial to your body. Especially when you live in a town where there are long lights and train crossings.

I also started mixing in affirmations with my *Autosize* workouts. I believe in affirmations, and have experienced first-hand how, when my mind is focused and positive, good things happen. As I started using the mind-body connection by mixing affirmations with the workouts, I noticed even more progress and toning would happen much faster. Also, the rest of my muscles started working in perfect harmony with my newly exercised muscles. I carried myself better. I had a better attitude. And I started loving my life more enthusiastically. Now I had found a workout that not only worked out my body, but also my mind.

## Barbara's Story

One of the people with whom I shared my *Autosize* workout was my goddaughter, Barbara. Barbara was an actress and model, and held the title of Mrs. California. She was used to being in great shape. She was also used to eating huge amounts of food, and not gaining weight. But then, she got pregnant with her son. She put on quite a bit of weight, and before she could lose all that extra "baby weight," she got pregnant again, and gave birth to her wonderful little girl, and her small frame grew even bigger.

The next couple of years, she did nothing but take care of her two babies, fill her face with empty calories, and put even more weight on! One day, she said, "Saba, I don't know what I'm going to do. I just can't get to a gym, and all this extra weight just isn't me!" She was depressed about the way she looked and felt. Luckily, Barbara already knew about the mind-body connection, so all I had to do was to remind her to get back into the practice of using it.

We made up some affirmations that were perfect for her. Then we cut out some pictures of what she looked like when she was active and having fun before her pregnancies. We also included some from when she received her crown for Mrs. California. She put a couple of pictures in her car, and the rest around the house. I showed her the entire *Autosize* program I had created. I told her to repeat her affirmations for a week, and when she truly believed that this workout would work for her, she should start doing it.

Barbara got serious about the program and made some changes in the way she was eating. The affirmations worked to help her reevaluate how she did a lot of things in her life. I also came up with some ideas on how she could practice weightlifting by using her kids. She started lifting the kids in and out of the car as if they were weights. All those minutes of doing the workout in her car really paid off. It took a while, but with concentrated effort and a more balanced diet, she got her body back to where it had been before she got pregnant. Barbara's success became my first real proof that what I was doing could be passed on to others, and that it really worked!

## Another Success Story

One day, about ten years ago, we were getting central air put into our house. We got to talking to one of the salesmen that came to give us an estimate, and he shared his challenge of having a little pot belly. You

SABA MOOR-DOUCETTE

know that paunch that seems appear on guys from the ever-present world of "Where the heck did this come from?" Tom said he spent most of his time in his truck driving from job to job, and by the time he got home, the last thing he wanted to do was to go out again to the gym. "You should *Autosize*," I said. "What the heck is that?" was his reply. I told him about how I had created it, and I showed him a few of the exercises just for his stomach. In about three weeks, Tom came back to start the job. He told me how much better he felt, and how much tighter his gut was getting. "This stuff really works! You should write a book!", he raved. Tom shrunk his belly bulge in just three weeks. I knew then that this idea was just too good to keep to myself.

## The Power of Synchronicity (When Combined with Mind and Spirit)

I started every day with a meditation. I would also affirm my desires to create *Autosize*, the book. Then, I got busy writing. I used stick figures to show the correct way to do each of the exercises and took pictures of myself for the cover. Then I created the perfect affirmation to go along with each of the exercises. I printed a few books up at our local copy place and started sharing them with friends.

Then one day, a friend said, "Why don't you make a video that shows the muscle groups you use in *Autosize* and compare them to the workout you'd get using gym equipment?" I thought that was a great idea.

I asked my girlfriend, Ellen, to help me put it all together. She was the perfect one for me to bring on board for this endeavor. Ellen and I were in a visualization workshop at Centers for Spiritual Living at the time. This particular class would meet weekly, visualize, affirm, and ultimately manifest all kinds of things. It was an amazing group that demonstrated the magnified power of thinking together as a group.

Ellen knew someone at church who worked as a camera operator for a well – known TV show. We approached Gina, and it just so happened she wanted to start her own production company. She had to build a promotional reel for herself, so she agreed to shoot and edit the video for free. Gina joined us in our visualization and meditation, and the project took on an even more powerful energy.

Things were happening fast, and all of us were so grateful at how perfectly everything was coming together, that we decided to call our production team "Gratitude Works."

I had it in my mind to get someone with a fabulous body to show how we were working the same muscles you might work on the machines at a gym. I also wanted the bodybuilder to be a man, to show that *Autosize* was for everyone, not just for women. He would also have to speak well, because we were going to both be talking in the video. Ellen had a friend that she thought would be the perfect fit. Chris was not only a bodybuilder, but a successful actor too. He had played the part of George in the movie *George of the Jungle 2* and was in top shape. He loved the idea and agreed to come on board.

Chris had a friend who owned Push Private Fitness, a nearby gym. We approached his friend, Chad, and he loved the idea. And best of all, he agreed to let us use his gym for free, and to talk about the benefits of each exercise, and how it correlated directly to my exercises in *Autosize*!

Everything was happening even better than we visualized it.

We made a plan to meet at the at the gym for the shoot in a couple of days. Wardrobe wasn't planned, but I knew that Spirit was really in the house when I wore my red top and my gray pants with a red stripe down the sides, and Chris showed up with a gray top and red pants that had a gray stripe down the side! I asked my friend, Babs, to be an extra along with Chad. We had a lot of fun all day shooting the video.

After completing the video, it came to me that these exercises were meant to be done in the car. So, it was only logical to create a CD people could play in their car to accompany them while they "Autosized." Affirming that thought, I made a few calls, and attracted exactly what I needed to make the CD. Finally, I had the whole package.

I had gotten this far by uniting my mind and my desires with Spirit through meditation and affirmations. I had attracted all the right people, the right ideas, and the facilities I needed to put the package together. Now I had to start marketing *Autosize*.

## Working Through Limitations

I had no idea how to market *Autosize*, but I knew that I should start by seeking guidance through meditation. Also, I started affirming and visualizing. I visualized people buying my book. I visualized myself appearing on TV shows to talk about the success of the book. I learned all I could about marketing, so I wouldn't have to use an expensive marketing company. I put up a website and a Facebook page, and I spoke to everyone I could about *Autosize*. The vision was always in my mind. I could see the end result, but I couldn't figure out why it wasn't happening. Something was blocking this from manifesting. But what?

Time passed, and life continued to happen. I was trying to spend as much time as I could with my grandchildren. My husband, Jeff, and I finished our studies, and we became licensed practitioners with the Centers for Spiritual Living. We were teaching our "Life Play" workshops, which focused on finding your Spirit through improvisation, and I was running a production company. But *Autosize* never left my mind. Why couldn't I get it off the ground?

One day, while organizing the garage, I bent over to pick up a small cardboard box with only a sweatshirt in it, and bam! I was stuck. Not only could I not stand up, I was in the worst back pain I've ever felt. The pain lasted for a few more days, and I still couldn't stand up or walk without extreme pain. For months I tried chiropractors, ancient Chinese herbs and treatments, and pain pills. Still no change. I was convinced I could handle this without a doctor, but the pain was too much.

Finally, I agreed to an MRI, and discovered that I had three slipped discs in my lower back, and two of them were ruptured as well. I resigned myself to riding around on one of those electric powered scooters, and for about a year, that's what I did.

One day, at a family get-together, one of my step-daughters told me how she got rid of a terrible upper back pain she had. She mentioned a book called *Healing Back Pain* by John Sarno, MD, a world renowned back expert.

Being a spiritual practitioner, I didn't always want to hear what medical doctors had to say, but I sat up and paid attention. I had heard about this book two other times over the last year, and the third time was the charm. On the way home, Jeff and I stopped at a local bookstore and bought the book.

Surprisingly, the book focused on the mind-body connection, and that was right up my alley. It showed me how there was no medical reason for my pain, despite the X-rays and the slipped and ruptured discs. To heal myself, I had to find out what the thought was that was being repressed and causing all my pain.

I examined my thoughts and feelings, and realized that I was more disappointed than I thought. I had been carrying this gigantic burden in trying to get *Autosize* off the ground. It was a psychological burden so great that it had literally crippled me. I took my psychological pain, and subconsciously transferred it to my lower back. The pain of not being as successful as I had hoped, and the inability to move forward with *Autosize*, was manifesting literally as the inability to walk and stand up straight.

Once I knew the truth, as if by magic, I was able to stand and walk a few steps without pain. I watched a video by Dr. Sarno, an elderly doctor in his eighties, wearing a lab coat, and holding a long rubber-tipped pointer just like my teachers used in grade school. He was making so much sense. By the end of the video, I was out of pain, and up and walking for good. I sold the scooter, and never looked back. I had learned a terrific lesson in the power of the mind. Every thought manifests as something. In my case, my thoughts of struggle and failure manifested as a crippling thought.

Over the years, whenever I feel a pain anywhere in my body, I take a serious inventory of my thoughts. Without fail, I can point to some limiting thought that was the cause of my pain. The mind is such a powerful instrument, and capable of so much more than we realize. This mind-body connection is one of the foundations of this book.

What I realized was that the mind-body connection also applies to suppressed and repressed emotions that manifest as overeating, lack of energy, and a limited view of our bodies.

We first think it, then we do it, and finally we become it.

## Becoming a Bikini Diva

After I got rid of that awful back pain, I even started dancing again. I was playing ball games with my grandchildren, and back to normal in every way. My best friend, Babs, started competing as a Bikini Diva. She had lost thirty-five pounds and wanted to hold herself accountable. She found a competition that was family-friendly and tested the competitors to make sure no drugs or steroids were being used. When she first told me about it, I thought it was kind of silly. Yes, I'm admitting it. I was judgmental.

I went anyway because I wanted to support her. And I was surprised when I met some of the competitors. The women competing were made up of teachers, moms, doctors, and one of the women was even a superior court judge. Wow, that sure taught me a lesson in pre-judging other people. We do learn through life lessons, don't we?

Babs had really toned her body in her year of preparation. I hardly recognized her up there on that stage. It was all very impressive. The competitions are done in categories. Babs was fifty-seven at the time, so she competed in the 50-59 year old age range. To our amazement, she took home a first place trophy!

After that, she tried to talk me into competing with her. "Think how much fun we would have together," she would constantly say to me. I just didn't think competing was for me.

A short while after her big win, Babs and I were talking about *Autosize*, and how I could market it. She said something that got my attention. "Maybe if you competed, you could get some credibility in the fitness field, and it would be easier to market it."

I know she said that sentence in a normal voice, but I heard it as loud as can be. It made so much sense to me. This was one of the things that had been blocking the success of *Autosize*. In that moment, I realized that I was just someone who came up with a cool idea for a workout. But what if I became a Bikini Diva or Sports Model? Then I would have credibility in the fitness field, and people would be more open to hearing what I had to say.

The first thing I did was to share my decision with Jeff. He was always a good barometer for my ideas. He would tell me if it was a good or a bad idea. I spoke to him, and he thought it was a good idea, and that I should go for it. I made up my mind that day to start working out and doing whatever I needed to do to get in good enough shape to compete as a Bikini Diva and Sports Model.

Because of my background in show business, I told Babs that If I'm going to do this, we should document it. And so, we did. We created a web series with the two of us learning how to best become Bikini Divas and Sports Models.

We had so much fun pointing out our strengths and deficiencies, while at the same time learning how to overcome those deficiencies and emphasize our strengths.

Like a sponge, I was soaking up all the information I could on the subject of health and fitness. If only I was like this in school, I would have been a straight A student! I was reading bodybuilding magazines, doing research on the internet, and asking female personal trainers how they get their bodies to look so firm and still feminine. I can remember the day I asked one of the trainers who had an exceptionally beautiful and toned body, how she got that way. She told me she worked out with weights and ate "clean." I had never heard that expression before. What the heck was "eating clean"? Ah, more to research.

Change definitely didn't happen overnight. I quickly learned that I had to change my eating and drinking habits if I wanted to have the body of my dreams. On the good side of the ledger, I was a thin person to start with, and I figured all I would have to do to get into shape was to work out extra hard, lift a few weights to lift my boobs a little, and take a few dance classes, so my butt would stop sagging. But when I actually started to do it, I realized what a huge challenge I had taken on, and doubt started to creep in.

I decided to deal with my doubts in my morning meditations. From my experience, all fears and doubts are more manageable when my mind is quiet. I made up affirmations and posted them up in various places around the house. I cut out a picture of a champion bikini competitor I wanted to look like and taped it on one of the shelves in the fridge. Every time I opened the fridge door, I would look at that picture and say, "That is what I will look like when I reach my goal!"

The next step was to eliminate any doubts about my age being a hindrance of any kind. These doubts had started to creep in, and make my goal seem harder to reach. It took a while, but I strengthened my belief by using affirmations to convince me that I would and could reach that goal.

Now, if you're thinking that it was easy for me since I was already thin, let me enlighten you to my lifestyle at the time. I loved going to the gym, but just for the Zumba, yoga, and other various classes they offered. I enjoyed the steam, sauna, and jacuzzi, but I never used any of the weights. As far as food went, I ate anything that looked or tasted good. I loved ice cream, especially jamoca almond fudge, and Pepsi was my favorite drink. I was a big meat-eater and loved baked or mashed potatoes with plenty of butter and sour cream. In & Out hamburgers, with a large order of fries, was my favorite quickie meal, and pizza with everything on it was a regular at our house. I was also a big bread eater, and I loved pasta with meatballs and sausage, cream sauce, or just plain butter. French toast or pancakes with syrup, bacon, and eggs was a typical Sunday breakfast. At least three times a week I would eat a bagel with lox and cream cheese. All meals were served on extra-big plates. When something was especially yummy, my husband and I both would have seconds. I could eat it all without gaining much weight, but my skin was sagging, my eyes had dark circles under them, and I had no muscle tone or endurance. I would not recommend my former diet to anyone.

At first, I made small changes. I thought I was really making a big commitment when I switched from Pepsi to Diet Pepsi. I cut down on the ice cream, which I had at least six times a week, to two times a week. I stopped eating candy and replaced it with health bars. I discovered the wrap so I could eat my hamburgers without the bun. The "wrap" is a hamburger wrapped in a big piece of lettuce instead of a bun.

I did a lot of changing in that first year of competing, but mostly with my mind. To stay on track, I had to constantly reinforce my decision to change my body with affirmations and visualizations. I also started being grateful every time I made a choice to eat the right things. It paid off. To my amazement, I won my first competition! I was officially a champion Bikini Diva.

After that, I was confident, and each goal I completed gave me more confidence. With that kind of momentum, I decided to really change the way I ate and lived my life. I completely eliminated diet soda, all dairy products, and sugar. No more ice cream, candy, Pepsi, or cake. I also cut way down on pasta, and eliminated white rice and white potatoes. I found other grains that were healthier and more nutritious, and even found some pre-cooked packages of healthy grains at Costco that were perfect for when I didn't want to cook on the stovetop. I started eating plenty of vegetables with lean meat and fish.

I felt stronger and healthier than I had ever felt. My skin was also taking on a healthier, more youthful look. Everywhere I went, people of all ages were asking me how I did it. I was giving advice from my own personal experience to everyone, but did I really know what I was talking about?

Not wanting to hurt anyone with wrong advice, Babs and I decided to take the journey of becoming certified personal trainers together. We studied hard for almost a year, and at age seventy, I became a Certified Personal Trainer. So, with all that knowledge, and three first place wins by age seventy, I reevaluated my goals. Instead of just getting in shape, my goal now was to bring all this knowledge to as many people as I could. I would continue to stay on the top of my game and share what I'd learned while becoming a Bikini Diva/Sports Model.

I started on this journey to monetize *Autosize*. But what I had become was an expert in the field of health, fitness, and anti-aging. At seventy-one, I looked back at everything I had done, and realized it all started with a thought, an idea. Through affirmations the thought turned into a belief, and the belief turned into an action, and, ultimately, became a lifestyle. I had become the very manifestation of health, beauty, and anti-aging.

It was only natural for me to create a workshop to share all this knowledge with as many people as I could. I called it "Staying Fit for Life with Saba's Think It, Do It, Be It Method." There was nothing blocking me now. I let go of how it was going to happen, and instead, allowed it to happen. I trusted my own mind, and the workings of Spirit that arose to support my new mindset. There is a saying by Mahatma Gandhi, "You must become the change you want to see in your life." I had become fit and healthy through affirmations, visualizations, and meditation. I now believed it thoroughly, and I was living it day by day.

## Ellen's Story

One day my older sister Ellen, who noticed what was going on with me, started a conversation with me about her weight challenge. Ellen, we finally discovered, is a highly functioning autistic. So highly functioning, you wouldn't even notice it unless you spent some time with her. Understanding a concept takes her a lot longer than your average person.

Ellen had put on quite a lot of weight over the years. She used to stuff her face with fattening foods and desserts, seconds, and sometimes thirds! Of course, this stretched her stomach and left her wanting more to fill the void. The whole family was on her about taking better care of herself, but nothing was getting through. She wanted to change the way she ate, but just couldn't get the concept. Every holiday for years I would say to her, "Are you sure you want to put that into your mouth?" She would laugh and say, "Oh, it's okay. I'm going to the gym tomorrow." I would often make jokes about her consumption of food. We would wind up laughing, but that never stopped her habitual overeating.

She finally developed diabetes and lost a lot of her energy. But that didn't stop her from eating what she shouldn't and gaining even more weight. This went on for years. Finally, two years into my competing, when I was seventy-one, and she was seventy-six, she asked, "How are you doing this? How can you change your body so much at this age, and not be tempted by everything on the table, and not eat chocolate?" I explained to her that I don't keep my eyes on the tantalizing spread before me. Instead, I keep my eyes on the future and what I can become. To my surprise, she was interested. She actually cared to talk about it. I was shocked. Without realizing it, I was setting an example. She had seen my competition pictures and was impressed with my physical changes. She also had been watching me and became aware of my healthy food choices at our family food fests.

For the first time in years, we had a serious talk with no jokes. I told her if she wanted to change her life, she had to seriously change her thinking. She knew all the concepts of affirming and visualizing, she just never practiced it with her body in mind. I told her if she was serious about getting healthy again, she would have to listen, really listen to what I had to say.

She seemed ready for a change in her life, so I gave her the affirmations that I thought would fit what she was about to do. I told her to use them for a week before she made any changes, and to write down everything she ate that week.

To my surprise, she did everything I told her to do. By the end of the week she was ready to get rid of everything that was stopping her from reaching her goal. She was excited, and so was I. She decided to be vegan to start, which shocked me, but I didn't negate her choice. I just supported her every way I could. She followed the Think It, Do It, Be It process to a tee. Within two years she lost four dress sizes. Now, four years later, she's no longer a vegan, but Ellen eats sensibly, and has lost over eighty pounds. She is eighty now, comfortable with her body. She loves going to her dances and having the energy to do the things she used to when she was younger.

Soon after that, I started to teach workshops privately and at the Center for Spiritual Living. The Think It, Do It, Be It method worked for everyone who committed to it. I continued to compete, and Spirit kept surprising me along the way. Out of the blue, Babs and I were offered to do a segment about health, fitness, and anti-aging on the nightly TV show, *Extra*. Then, a London producer contacted me about doing a segment on a docu-comedy special featuring Mickey Flanagan, a very funny British comedian. They had found my website and thought it would be fun for Mickey to actually learn how to do *Autosize* for himself. They came to Los Angeles, and we spent the day driving around town talking and laughing, while I taught Mickey how to *Autosize*. Spirit had taken over completely, and now things were happening without me even trying.

Then one day, Bill and Gayle Gladstone were discussing an online network that they were putting together. Their daughter-in-law overheard them, and said, "Oh my gosh! You guys have got to meet Saba! She would be perfect for this!" She went on about me for a while, and they seemed slightly interested. When Bill's son came into the room and asked, "Are you talking about Saba? Oh Dad, you would love her. She's absolutely amazing, and just what you are looking for." Now they had Bill's full attention.

Natasha was just a young producer when we met eight years before. Even though she wasn't an actress, I talked her into playing a part in our web series. She was perfect for the part. I coached her and took her under my wing. We became very close, and over the years, I tried to help her in any way I could. Now eight years later, it was Natasha and her husband Cyrus's pitch that led to this book.

My advice to you is to have fun with this book. Allow change into your life. Be willing to try things you've never considered before or were always afraid to try. Learn how powerful you can be by training your mind to cooperate with your dreams.

It took me twenty-five years, after the first thought I had to create *Autosize,* to manifest this book. That alone should tell you that it's never too late. And as far as I'm concerned, you are never ever allowed to give up on your dreams! You may not know how they will happen, but if you stay focused on keeping the dream alive, and build up your belief in it through affirmations, visualizations, and actions, there is no way you can fail.

Think It. Do It. Be It. And anyone can be Fit for Life.

## What is *THINK IT, DO IT, BE IT?*

## Think It

If you want to live a healthy lifestyle and create a body to match the image of that lifestyle, you've got to eliminate any unhealthy thoughts and habits that don't contribute to that image. Step one of this program focuses on training your mind through the use of affirmations, visualizations, meditation, and journaling, to think healthy thoughts that empower you to create positive changes in your life. Everything depends on the power of your thoughts.

## Do It

Take action. Just thinking about something is nice, but it doesn't get things done. In the Do It section of this book, you will be shown specific ways to combine your actions with your new way of thinking by focusing on the steps needed to change your body. Specific ideas on diet and exercise will help you develop new healthy habits that lead to a life of fitness and ageless beauty.

## Be It

Simply put, you will become the embodiment of this new vision of yourself. You will feel the presence of health and beauty from within. In every conscious thought and action, you will reflect the most beautiful version of you.

Welcome to *Think it. Do it. Be it.*

# CHAPTER 2:
# THINK IT – BUILDING THE
# MIND/BODY CONNECTION

Everything you've experienced and believed about your experience has led you to where you are in your life right now. You become what you think and believe. So, if you think of yourself as out of shape, over-weight, undisciplined, ugly, incompetent, lazy, stupid, or anything else, you will become exactly that. So, how has that been working for you?

If you want to affect change in your life, you have to start at the source: your thoughts. So, let's start by changing what we think and believe about our bodies, diet, exercise, and the new possibilities that are open to you.

## Developing New Habits

When I teach my workshops, I suggest that the time it takes to incorporate this program and create new habits properly is three weeks. There is a learning curve needed when you start changing your thinking to absorb new information and develop new habits. Everyone is different. I know one or two people who make up their minds, and that's it. They're done with the old habit, and on to a new one. This type of rigid discipline is extremely rare, however. Most need a longer period of time to retrain their mind and develop a new physical habit. Just think of all the other times you tried to change your diet, give up smoking, start a new exercise program, or adapt to a new job or a new routine of any kind.

I suggest that it will take you a minimum of three weeks to really feel and incorporate the changes this program will create in your life. Three weeks will give you the time you need to make a start in building new behaviors. You need to strengthen your mind-muscle as you experience and incorporate personal changes, and adapt to the new vision of beauty, health, and exercise you are creating for yourself.

As you go along, you may find yourself "slipping" here and there, reverting to old behaviors and habits. Maybe your schedule interferes, or maybe an old pattern rears up and grabs you. Don't get discouraged. It happens. The important thing is not to beat yourself up over a "slip," but to accept it as part of a process, and move on with the program again. Anger, frustration, or self-loathing in any way will only cause you to love yourself less and make the process that much more difficult. The more you love yourself through the process, the easier it will be to change. If you slip, rededicate yourself and affirm:

*I am changing my life one moment at a time. This event has shown me the right way to love myself and move forward from this moment on.*

## Your Thoughts Create Your World

In the beginning was the word. The word, in this case, stands for your thought. Nothing can take form without thinking about it first. The Think It, Do It, Be It process obviously starts with what you are thinking. You undoubtedly have a lot of negative ideas that have built up over the years about getting fit and healthy. To move past negative thoughts, you have to start changing how you think about yourself, and your relationship to diet and exercise. The Think It, Do It, Be It method is built on sound scientific principles. If you aren't familiar with the value of affirmations, let me say a little about it.

It has long been known that where the mind goes, the body follows. You can't even pick up your coffee cup without your mind first telling your muscles to do it. The mind conceives, and the body achieves. Just willing your body to do something that you don't believe will only achieve mediocre results. What you're doing soon becomes tiring, and boredom sets in making all your efforts counter-productive. I want you to not only have fun through the process of change, but also be inspired.

Most of our thoughts are unconscious. We don't consciously think about telling our hand to pick up the coffee cup. We just do it. It happens almost instantaneously. Unfortunately, through much of our lives we are telling ourselves to do things from an unconscious level of thinking. Truth be told, much of what we tell ourselves, both consciously and unconsciously, is not doing us any good, and is only contributing to limiting our success in many areas, including weight loss and fitness. A fantastic way to start bringing your thoughts up to a conscious level and making sure they are positive and constructive thoughts is to start doing affirmations.

## Affirming Your Way to Health

Simply stated, affirmations are positive thoughts you say aloud that reinforce the kind of thoughts you want to think, and the life you want to experience in your conscious mind. The more you repeat them, the more real they become for you. In turn, the more real they become for you, the more your life changes to match the direction of your affirmative thoughts. They're easy to do, and you will be amazed at how much they will change your thinking, and therefore, your life.

When you start doing these affirmations, you will find joy and purpose in what you are doing. That will go a long way in keeping you on track and feeling successful. This step is most likely what has been missing from all your past diets and attempts to get in shape. So, let's start building a strong foundation that will help keep you on point for the rest of your life.

I want you to look at this list of affirmations and pick at least three of them to start repeating to yourself throughout the day for the first week.

*I am excited about taking action toward being fit.*
*I can do this program one day at a time.*
*I am in control of my choices.*
*I make healthy choices for myself.*
*Today, I drop all judgment of myself and others.*

*I am grateful for this wonderful day.*
*I deserve to be happy and healthy.*

Make sure you repeat them in the morning, afternoon, and at bedtime. The more you repeat them throughout your day, the more effective they will be. If you can do all six, even better.

Do whatever you need to remember them. Write them down and carry them with you so you can repeat them anytime during the day. Repeat them in the car, in the elevator, in the bathroom, while doing dishes, or any time you can. Post them on your bathroom mirror, on the front of the refrigerator, and at various places around your home, and keep a copy of them with you at all times.

Notice what your reaction is to these affirmations. Do you believe them? Do they make you feel hopeful? More joyous? More accepting of yourself?

Or

Do they bring up a little nagging doubt? What's the thought in your head that makes you doubt them? Where did that thought come from? Is that thought serving you or limiting you?

Write down some of your thoughts, but don't get bogged down in anything negative. Just keep it simple and factual. Write down your reactions and keep monitoring those reactions. See if they start lessening or becoming bigger obstacles. Later, we'll explain how to work through these observations in the journaling section. But for now, just list them quickly and go about your business.

---

**TIP**
**Record yourself saying your affirmations,**
**so you can repeat them along with yourself**
**in your car, on a walk, or anywhere else.**

---

One of the tools I have found to be very helpful in the practice of changing my thoughts, is to listen to inspirational recordings of speakers and books while I'm driving around in my car. When you surround yourself with positive thoughts wherever you go, negative thinking turns into positive thinking with much more ease. By doing this you put yourself in the process of building a strong mental attitude that will assist you in accomplishing your goals. You are building the strongest and most powerful muscle you have ... your mind-muscle.

When you are healthy and strong in both your body and mind, there will be no stopping you from achieving any goal you set for yourself. My goal was to go from a fairly thin senior citizen with a saggy aging body, to a Bikini Diva/Sports Model. I didn't even start until I was sixty-eight years old. And look at what I accomplished as a result. Now I'm in my seventies, and I'm still doing it. And you can do it too.

Goals help you focus. They help to strengthen your mind-muscle, and that is what the Think It part of the process is all about. You need to sit down and figure out what your goals actually are. Are you going for weight loss? A healthier diet? Or getting totally fit? For example, if you are going to lose weight, decide how may pounds you would like to lose, and how long you want to take to lose them. It's important to be realistic. Obviously, you can't lose twenty pounds a week and stay healthy, but two to five pounds a week is definitely doable depending on your body type. You can always change your goal as you become more comfortable with the process, and as you find your mind getting stronger.

To start, ask yourself what kind of body you would have if you lived in a world with no limits. Got it? Okay, now come back to earth. If you set a goal that is unrealistic, chances are pretty good that you will never achieve it.

Now take a look at yourself in the mirror, and truly see what is looking back at you. Try to stick with reality, but remove all judgement of that reality. Tell that little nagging voice in your head to be still for a moment while you honestly evaluate the situation. If you're short and overweight, okay, that's fine. It is what it is. If your hips are really large, okay, that's fine. It is what it is. It's unrealistic for most of us to wish we were leggy blonde models who weigh almost nothing, when we're really only five feet tall. Besides, that's just marketing. The more manufacturers can make you feel inadequate, the more they can sell you clothes and products that promise to make you look better, attract sexual partners, and be more successful. Again, let's look at the truth. You are more than your body, and who you are is beautiful, if you choose to see that beauty.

Now look at yourself again, and really try to see the beautiful things about you. Focus on what you really like, not what you don't like. If you find yourself going negative, gently pull yourself back to something positive. This can be the first step in beginning to love yourself the way you should be loved.

When you've started feeling better about yourself, look at yourself again, and try to see more realistically what you need to change immediately. Keep it positive. See a version of you that is attainable and would make you feel great. Maybe it's just a little thinner here and there, or a size or two smaller dress or waist size. That's fine for now. Goals can always be adjusted and reimagined. It's better to start with something attainable, so that you feel encouraged when you actually attain it, instead of feeling discouraged by not being able to reach some unrealistic ideal.

For any goal to work, you have to truly believe you can attain it. Remember what Henry Ford said, "Whether you think you can or whether you think you can't, you're right." Ford was a very positive thinker. He had an idea to build his car and develop a way to mass produce it for others. Even though he got nothing but negatives from most people, he forged ahead not letting anything stop him from his dream. He succeeded because he built a consciousness which believed that no matter what, he was going to succeed. That is the consciousness this program will help you develop. If you don't believe in what you are doing one hundred percent, don't tell anyone about it until you do. Even then, it's better not to tell others. No matter how well meaning, you will hear a lot of bad advice, negative inference, or suggestions that will discourage you, and keep you from reaching your goal. Remember, it doesn't matter what anyone else thinks about what you are doing for yourself. You have to know at the very core of your being that you can do this. Beyond wishing or even believing is knowing. Remember, whether you think you can or you think you can't you are right! So, choose a goal, and know you are going to reach it.

## Partnering

My step-daughter wrote a diet and exercise book years ago called *The Game-On Diet.* In it, she challenged people to "partner up." She loves games, so she wanted to create a diet that had a level of competition in it.

Amazing results can be achieved when you have someone to support or push you, but not necessarily compete against you. Having someone you can honestly discuss your challenges with is an excellent idea. You can support each other by making goals, and going through challenges together. You can push each other, check in on each other, and celebrate the attainment of your goals with each other.

## Rewards

Whether you do the program alone or with a partner, it's important to reward yourself when you achieve a goal. If you are doing this program alone, then just treat yourself to something. Buy a new piece of clothing or take yourself out to a good restaurant for a really tasty healthy meal. Enjoy what you are doing. Make it a fun, rewarding practice.

# If You Don't Like It, Change It

One of my students wanted to lose some weight. Kathy set her goals and started working towards them. She stated how much she wanted to lose, and how long it would take her. She was repeating her affirmations, and visualizing the pounds dropping off. Getting a clear picture of what she wanted to look like when she reached her goal was blocking her from moving forward. After a week, she started to doubt if she could really reach her goal. We talked about it and came up with a vision of the dress that she wanted to fit into. She changed her goal from a specific figure she wanted, which seemed like something she couldn't realistically imagine, to a picture of her fitting into that dress. That she could see. She bought the dress, and hung it outside of her closet where she could see it daily. She started visualizing herself at her high school reunion dancing, having fun, and looking fantastic in that dress. Changing her goal to something more specific and exciting that she could easily see was the perfect choice for her.

# Visualizations

Affirmations and visualizations go hand in hand. Visualizing is something we do all the time. We imagine pictures and scenes that are only in our mind.

Creative visualization is using these imaginative pictures as an inspirational guide to creating what you want in your life. Imagining your body looking the way you would like it, or fitting into the clothes you love, are wonderful visualizations. Maybe you want to visualize the scale dropping to the desired weight you are seeking, or perhaps picture yourself working out and developing a perfect set of six-pack abs. Anything you can imagine will work for you. The successful ones in life spend a lot of time daydreaming or visualizing success. On the other hand, many spend far too much time seeing themselves as unworthy, or living in a fearful world. Which would you rather imagine for yourself?

What I want you to do now is to visualize the body you want to have. Use your imagination. Visualize what you will look like when you finally reach your goal. Get a clear picture of it in your mind. Visualize that image for yourself throughout the day. Add to it, or change it as you wish, but keep imagining.

If you find you are having a challenge with this, it will help you if you cut out a picture of someone with the body that looks like the one you desire. You can even paste your face on that body if it helps. Or, find an old picture of yourself when you were at your perfect weight. Keep the picture where you can see it often and take the time to consciously look at it for a minute or so whenever possible. Put that picture on your cell phone, or carry a small copy in your wallet or purse, and look at it. Repeat the affirmations, and get excited about what you are doing.

When I first started changing my body, I cut out a picture of a Bikini Diva champion from a few years ago, and taped it inside my refrigerator. So, every time I opened the door, there it was to remind me of my goal. Every once in a while, I would look at that picture and doubts would arise, but I would immediately start repeating my affirmations, and picture myself the way I wanted to be. It worked, and the stronger I developed that mind-muscle, the quicker it worked.

## Put Some Feeling into Your Visualizations

Throughout the day, try closing your eyes and imagine feeling the way you would love to feel, and doing things that you would like to do when you're in shape. Maybe you're on the beach in a new swimsuit, or getting compliments at your school reunion. Maybe you're being more active with your kids and/or grandchildren, or fitting into those "skinny pants" you've been hanging onto.

Feel the feelings, and see the results in your mind. Smile, laugh, let your heart race a little. The clearer the picture and the more intense the feeling, the more you will transform into your new consciousness.

## Vision Boards

Vision boards can be a lot of fun to create. If you are artistic, you can draw or paint pictures of what you desire for your outcome. Although my mother and my granddaughter are artists, that talent must have skipped a generation, because I can barely draw a stick figure. So, in my case I decided to cut pictures out of magazines, or print them from the internet, and paste them onto a poster board. I would pick pictures of Bikini Divas receiving awards for their wins, a woman at a book signing for her #1 best seller, a star sitting on the panel of a TV show, or a speaker in front of large crowds. I cut out a picture of myself and a car, and then pasted the picture of me in the car. Then I wrote *Autosize: #1 Workout of the Year* under the picture and put it where I could see it every day. Those were my desires for the perfect outcome. Then I wrote the perfect affirmations for myself, and put them on top of each picture.

---

**Tip**
Make your own vision board. Find some old pictures of the way you used to look, or cut out pictures from magazines that closely resemble your desired goal. Maybe pictures on the beach, dancing, or playing a sport. Then write the affirmations that make you feel good, and put them around your board. Be creative. Have fun!

---

## Guided Meditations

There are many guided meditations available for free on the internet, or you can buy them on CDs. They take you on little imaginary trips into consciousness by describing or suggesting pictures for you to imagine. They relax the mind, body, and soul. When your mind goes to a certain deep space in your guided meditation, you can easily picture yourself the way you want to be, with the body you want, and doing the things you desire. The images you create in these meditations are very powerful. They make a deep impression on your subconscious mind, and implant a positive image at that deep level. They work in similar ways as hypnosis, but you're doing it yourself. You can even create your own guided meditation with images that work really well for you. Just listen to one or two, and you'll get the idea.

You can visualize with your eyes open or closed, in a comfortable chair, or on your bed or couch. Just as long as you are not disturbed by anyone or anything.

## Sample Meditation #1

Close your eyes, and take three deep breaths. With each breath, relax every part of your body. When you're fully relaxed, imagine taking yourself to a favorite safe place. It might be a beautiful beach where you can hear the sound of the waves crashing or gently washing up onto the shore. You might choose a secret place in a forest, or next to a rippling creek, or the top of a mountain, where the wind is gently blowing, or even out on a lake in a rowboat. It's your choice, but spend time enjoying that place, and really feeling it in your mind and body. Now, imagine yourself at your perfect weight and shape approaching you. Smile as you recognize yourself, and appreciate how well you did to achieve that perfect shape. You could have an imaginary conversation with your transformed self, and find out how you did it, or how you got through certain challenges. After your conversation, give your "other self" a huge hug, and release her/him to go on to the perfect life you want. As you watch your "other self" leave, be grateful for what you will soon become. Take a minute or so to come out of the meditation, and reconnect to the space around you. Write down any insights, and make a promise to yourself to go back again soon.

## Sample Meditation #2

First get comfortable. Notice how you are breathing. Take three deep breaths, and relax into them. Don't try to force yourself to feel relaxed. Just feel whatever you are feeling, and focus on releasing. Your feelings might be something you can journal about later, but for now, just try to relax through those feelings. Soon you will notice every part of your body relaxing.

Picture your body as it is now. Really take it in, without any judgment, just as it is. As you picture yourself, repeat these affirmations:

> *I am perfect the way I am right now.*
> *I see myself getting healthier and more fit*
> *every day. I accept change with ease.*
> *Whatever I envision, I can do.*

Now imagine you are in the body you desire. See a close friend, a spouse, a family member, or someone who is very supportive in your life. Imagine hearing and feeling their loving support. What are they saying? Enjoy it for a while. Smile. Love that support.

Now move on to some acquaintance who is not as close to you personally. It might be a person at the gym, the checkout person at the store, or almost anyone you run into from time to time. Imagine their face as they see you in your new body. Let yourself be surprised as they tell you how good you look. What are they saying? Enjoy it. Love it. Smile, and be grateful. Wallow in the joy you feel as you see yourself in your mind. What you see will become a reality, and everything you just imagined is about to happen for real.

Allow this meditation to sit with you for a minute. Take one or two deep breaths, and come out of the meditation feeling refreshed and strong.

If you can't remember the steps, record them on your phone or any other recording device. If you like, you can put on some soothing noninvasive meditation background music.

## Sample Meditation #3

If you choose to visualize with your eyes open, look at your vision board, or the clothes you will be fitting into as soon as you reach your goal. Let your mind run free with all of the places you will go, and all the things you will do. You are thinking in pictures. Some people will call this daydreaming.

Whether your eyes are opened or closed, allow yourself to smile. Enjoy what you are envisioning. Know that what you are doing for yourself is helping you to actually be the person you want to be!

## Journaling

Journaling has been proven to be one of the most effective ways to explore your subconscious, and work through problems of the conscious mind. It unleashes new levels of thinking by tapping into the right brain which is the creative side of the brain. Besides acting as a chart for your progress and the changes you are going through, it is an excellent way for your subconscious mind to express previously unexpressed fears, inspirations, past grievances, and memories that might be acting as limitations to your progress.

I always write my journals out longhand. Typing a journal does not have the same effect as writing. The physical act of writing is a left-brain activity. The left brain is the logical and orderly side of the brain. The right hemisphere of the brain is the creative, intuitive side. The left side of the brain loves to be strict, to judge, to see only one way of doing things. The right brain loves to create, to fill in blanks, to be more unruly and adventurous. When we occupy the left brain with a familiar task, the right brain is free to roam, to discover, to inspire.

Have you ever noticed how when you're driving, doing dishes, taking a shower, or doing any familiar task, you are often hit with brilliant insights and ideas? That's the right brain talking to you. The same phenomenon occurs when you are writing out your thoughts longhand. Your left brain is occupied with the familiar task of writing, and freeing up your right brain to talk to you, reveal things, solve problems, and create strategies for you.

There's not many rules to follow. Try to write at least a page or two every day, and more is never a bad thing. I've used legal pads, spiral notebooks, free pages, and every other variation. None of that matters. The secret is to keep the hand moving even if you don't think you have much to say. When I do it, I often end up writing things like "I don't have anything to say. I'm done. No thoughts. What could I possibly write to keep my hand moving? This is a lame exercise." Then, this kind of thing happens, "Wait, I'm judging this process. I judge a lot, and it's not good for me ... etc." Out of nothing comes a revelation that will help you to progress. Just keep the hand moving. Even if you come up with nothing new, keep going. Eventually, your subconscious and your right brain will discover this avenue of communication, and start revealing tremendous insights.

Stay away from dwelling on negative things, especially when it comes to working the program. When a negative thought comes up, notice it, write it down, and immediately move on. Your subconscious has already noted it, and is working on finding how to overcome it. By dwelling on the negative, we encourage more of the same. What you put your attention to attracts similar thoughts. So, put your attention on discovery and resolution.

Problems don't get solved by focusing on the problem, but by accepting a new thought about it that both releases the problem, and allows you to move forward. And always remember to praise your successes. Give yourself credit, and write about how well you're doing, how well you're feeling, and how much better you look.

As you journal, you will discover all kinds of things like:

- Why am I blocking my own progress?
- What's standing in my way?
- What kind of limiting thoughts do I have?
- Did someone tell me that, or did I create it?
- How much of that blockage am I responsible for? When did I choose to accept these limitations?

- Am I ready to release this thought, and accept another more positive one?
- Do I need to amend my goals to something more realistic?
- What new affirmations can I come up with to help me?

As you work your way through these questions, you will start seeing a new awareness about yourself developing. I will tell you now never to blame yourself or anyone else for your problems. The last thing we want is to create new resentments. Just accept the fact that you, and everyone else, was acting the only way you or they knew how. They have their problems. You have yours. We can all get rid of them if we allow ourselves to release our attachment to them. Journaling will help you to release and move forward, as well as, or better than, many sessions on a psychiatrist's couch. Journal daily. It's cheaper.

Below is a discovery I made while journaling. It is an example of how we often install our own limitations.

## We All Love Our Mothers, But ...

One day many years ago, I was journaling about being sick. I had been sick in bed with what seemed to be a never-ending cold. I felt as though I had a fever, but my temperature was normal. This was a common occurrence with me. When I was a kid In New York, I used to get sick all the time. We had our seasonal weather changes, and you could bet money that I would get sick at the change of each season. You would win that bet every time. I was fifteen when we moved to California, and I thought with all that fabulous warm weather, my days of getting sick were over. I was wrong. Getting sick became a pattern, and I got so used to getting sick, I never noticed or even questioned why It was happening.

One day years later, my daughter Syd, who was now an adult with children of her own, said to me, "Mom, why are you sick all the time?" It was at that point that I became aware of all the times I was sick. She was right, I was sick a lot. I also had headaches, and felt nauseous more often than any human should. I started keeping a record of each time I got sick during that year, and what it was I was suffering from. It blew me away how often I was down with one thing or another. What was going on with me?

I decided to journal. I asked myself all kinds of questions. At first the journaling didn't lead me to any solid answers, but I kept going. One day, out of the blue, I found myself writing about my childhood. I wrote about my mother's fear of the cold, and her fear of getting a chill, which surely would lead to a cold. All kinds of fears my mother had repeated to me growing up started to surface. They were nothing but old wives' tales, like catching a cold from a draft, or drowning if you went swimming after eating, but they had a profound effect on my little innocent creative mind. The flood gates opened up and all my mother's fears of what can get me sick started to fill the pages. It wasn't until I wrote for at least ten pages that I was hit with the realization of what had been going on with me for years. It's amazing how deep things can go, and how you can stuff them away never realizing the effect these false beliefs can have on your life.

SABA MOOR-DOUCETTE

Through journaling, I discovered why I was sick all the time. I loved my mother very much, and because of that, I wanted what she said to be right. In my mind, I was showing my mother that I loved her by getting sick from all of the things she had warned me about. Things that scientifically shouldn't really get you sick were making me sick. Once I realized that, I no longer had to get sick from being in a draft, getting wet in the rain, or just worrying too much. I got busy working on eliminating those false beliefs. With the help of hypnotherapy and lots of journaling, I was able to heal myself. Now, whenever I get sick, I try to figure out what's going on in my life. I usually get there quickly through meditation and journaling, and lo and behold, I am healthy once again.

Happily, I was actually able to talk to my mother about it. At first, she said, "Oh, so it's my fault you're sick?" Spoken truly like a Jewish mother. But after a lot of discussion, I made her understand that I wasn't blaming her, and I ended up teaching her how not to get sick when she gets a chill. I love being able to teach my mother new thought.

How many false beliefs about your body or your life do you cling to? Start journaling, and you'll find many things you never knew.

# CHAPTER 3:
# DO IT

You can do all of the thinking in the world, but if you don't take action nothing will happen for you. By now you know that the mind is the most powerful muscle we have. The stronger you can develop that muscle, the easier it will be for you to reach your goal.

Affirmations, visualizations, meditation, and journaling could be considered part of the Do It phase of the program, since they are actual steps you are taking. But they deal mostly with how you can change your mind. I know that changing your mind works because everyone I've ever worked with at home, in workshops, or in the gym, reports back to me how these techniques have changed their life. Now it's time for you to experience how the new mindset you're still developing makes it easier for you to step into the Do It phase.

## Taking Your Body on a Vacation

Congratulations! You have made it through your first week. You should be mentally charged up and ready to go. You are now ready for your first week of Doing It.

Keep your affirmations going this week, and let's use that energy to help strengthen your desire to reach your goal.

I love to compare getting your body in shape with taking a vacation. If you were going on a vacation to the Bahamas, you wouldn't pack a winter coat, long johns, or furry snow boots. Would you? Of course not! Consider that you are about to take your body on a vacation. Let's see what you should pack for the trip.

At the risk of stretching this vacation metaphor a little further, let's look and see what there is to pack. Your cupboards and fridge are the logical place to start.

## Going Through Your Cupboards

What kind of foods do you have in your cupboards? Our rule of thumb in packing for this vacation is for you to limit unnecessary items that only make your bags heavier. Don't add anything that you don't absolutely need for the vacation you're about to take.

## Note:

I understand that you might have a spouse, a roommate, kids, or relatives living in the same space. Of course, you have to think of their needs as well, but perhaps you can set aside a shelf or two in your kitchen just for you.

Tell everyone what you're doing. Let everyone know you will be putting some things on shelves and in containers that will be just for you. Ask them to help you with the process by being your support system. It always helps when you are accountable to someone else.

The first thing to do is to identify the stuff you know you don't want to take on your trip. You probably have a good idea what those things are already, but let's go over them anyway.

We're looking to eliminate chemicals and processed foods in general, and to start eating only fresh, non-processed foods. This is referred to as "eating clean."

# Eating Clean

If you've ever heard the term "eating clean" and didn't know what the heck it meant, don't feel bad. As I mentioned, when I started, I went around asking all of the female trainers that looked perfectly toned how they did it. Their first reply was, "I eat clean."

When I had heard that reply a few times, I finally asked one of the trainers what it meant. She explained that she didn't eat anything that's been processed. Nothing out of a box, frozen, or out of a can. That seemed a bit drastic to me, but then I would look at their sculpted, healthy-looking bodies, and think to myself, "Well, if that's what it takes, then that's what I'll have to do." I only had a few exceptions to that rule, which I will mention in the diet and shopping list section. But let me tell you, I had to read a lot of labels to find only a few exceptions.

# Sugar and Sugar Substitutes

Besides processed foods, get rid of sugar and sugar substitutes. At the very least, keep them out of sight if others in the household still use them.

What? No sweets?

Don't panic! You don't have to cut sweetness out of your life completely. I have created some recipes for sugarless sweets in the recipe section of this book that will satisfy your cravings. You can also find these recipes on my website www.ThinkitDoitBeit.us These other sweeteners will give you more energy, and help you to avoid the inevitable energy crash that comes with eating sugar and chemically based substitutes.

With healthier sweeteners, you'll be doing your body a big favor by avoiding spikes in energy and mood. Sure, sugar tastes great and feels great when you eat it, but that's because it literally acts like a drug in your system. And with that great feeling you get comes a big crash. It's when you're in the low points of that sugar cycle that you want to eat more and more junk to keep the high going. The same is true of too many quickly processed carbs like chips, non-whole grain bread, and most tropical fruits.

Again, if others in the house are not on board with you, tell them they can best support you by keeping that stuff out of sight until you've learned how to successfully make healthier choices in a world full of sugar. And that will happen. The healthier you get and the healthier you feel, the less you will desire anything that doesn't contribute to that feeling.

## Get Over the Sugar Habit

If you want to feel good and keep your energy balanced all day, I suggest you cut out anything with sugar or sugar substitutes. In no time your body will respond, and you will no longer have those sugar cravings.

> ### Tip
> **Consuming sugar for energy or for a
> mood lift is the worst habit you can get
> into. Sugar is in almost everything you
> buy, so be careful. Read labels.**

Not only has sugar been proven to be responsible for diabetes and other diseases, including cancer, heart disease, and obesity, it's also bad for your teeth, contains non-essential nutrients, and it's addictive. Besides its addictive qualities, sugar and foods that turn to sugar quickly in your bloodstream like chips, bread, crackers, pasta, and other non-whole grain flour products are one of the major causes of WRINKLES! Yes, wrinkles.

This is an interesting and fairly unknown tidbit. Anyone interested in anti-aging should care about that.

## Sugar Substitutes

Say goodbye to Sweet 'N Low, Equal, Sweet One, and Sugar Twin. Check out all packaged items, and get rid of any that include sugar, corn syrup, saccharin, dextrin, aspartame, dulci-tol, or mannitol, and any ingredient that ends in "ose." It's a good idea to stay away from processed packaged items in general as they include all kinds of chemicals, preservatives, hidden sugars, and other ingredients that do not contribute to a healthy lifestyle.

Stevia is available at most stores, and is just about the only sugar substitute that won't raise your glycemic index in any significant way. Small amounts of agave sweetener, honey, and molasses are acceptable unless you're a diabetic.

## Dairy

Personally, I don't consume milk products. Milk is processed, and therefore it's out of my diet, and should be out of yours. After doing a study on milk, I discovered that we humans are the only species that uses milk after early childhood. No other species consumes milk as an adult. A good thing to do for your body is to give up dairy products completely. I know this could be a hard thing for you if you love milk products like cheese or ice cream, but it could be one of the best things you do for your body. It was one of the best choices I ever made. Here are some humane and scientific reasons why you should cut milk out of your food choices:

- Most cows are pumped up with steroids so they can produce faster. This can throw off your hormonal balance.
- Most cows are fed with genetically-modified (GM) animal by-products that include antibiotics and pesticides.
- Drinking milk as an adult can throw off your metabolic balance.
- Most cows are raised in pens barely big enough to stand up in, attached to milking machines twice a day, impregnated through artificial insemination to keep them producing more milk, and have their calves ripped from them at birth. They never get to be free or roam on grass their entire life.

If you are a big dairy consumer and quit cold turkey, you will find you drop the weight even faster.

Soy milk and soy cheese are acceptable substitutes, along with almond milk, coconut milk, rice milk, and a few other non-dairy products.

Even knowing all of these facts, around the holidays, I still cheat with an open sandwich of half a bagel, lox, and cream cheese. Occasionally, I also put some Swiss cheese on my burger. Guess what? It didn't kill me! I was sure to affirm just before and while I was eating those treats that,

*A tiny cheat here and there will not keep me from reaching my goal.*

But remember, I only did this after I reached my desired weight. I knew that I had built up my mind-muscle and my daily eating habits to the point where I could trust myself, and know that what I was saying was true.

## Bread and Carbohydrates

When I started watching my food intake, the next thing that I did was to cut out bread. You'll be surprised at what a difference that will make in the way you feel. I also cut out all deep-fried or crusted food, and flour based foods in general. I would have the occasional rice cracker, but I emphasize "occasional."

Carbs are present in almost everything, including most veggies, but it's the "bad carbs" in most flour and sugar based products that are the worst. If you want to lose weight, limit your intake of bad carbs. It really isn't that hard once you learn how to eat clean and healthy.

Like most of you, I had a habit of turning to carbs for my snacks. Then I started eating raw veggies, seeds, and nuts for my crunch instead. Besides the crunch I was craving, I was getting some really good protein and other essential nutrients instead of just empty carbohydrates. And I didn't really miss those "bad carbs" at all.

After a while you will start feeling more energetic and clear-headed. As you learn to make healthier choices, avoiding bread and flour products will become easier and easier. Gradually, you will understand more about how food affects your entire being, and willingly eat clean and healthy. I promise.

After you learn how to communicate with your body better, you can add bread back into your diet here and there. Personally, I love sandwiches, and occasionally started eating open-faced sandwiches, using only one piece of bread. Then I started doing research on the different choices of healthy breads. I found a few that were heathy, but as far as taste goes, yuk. Then I found Dave's

---

**TIP**
**Only reintroduce small amounts of dairy and bread after you've reached your desired weight.**

---

**TIP**
**Make open-faced sandwiches. Use one slice of bread, and you will fool your body into thinking you had a regular sized sandwich. Or make a half sandwich, and put it on a very small plate.**

---

Killer Bread, the best tasting bread I've ever had. It is made with 21 whole grains and seeds, no high fructose corn syrup, no artificial preservatives, USDA organic, Non-GMO, and made with killer taste and texture.

## The List of What to Eliminate

Here are some other things you should eliminate:

- Sugary drinks
- Most pizzas-it's the dough that turns into sugar in your bloodstream
- Most commercial breads, especially white bread
- Most fruit juices. They are mostly sugar
- Industrial vegetable oils
- Margarine
- Pastries, cookies and cakes
- French fries
- Potato chips, corn chips, and any chips that aren't on my food list
- Candy
- Most desserts
- Anything canned or packaged with some exceptions like:

  Wild canned salmon in water
  Wild canned tuna in water
  Canned sardines and oysters Trader Joe's black beans Costco's instant madras lentils

- Packaged Seeds of quinoa with brown rice

# CHAPTER 4:
# DIET

This is more than just another diet book. It's meant to change the way you look at food and how you relate to it in general. I want to show you a way of eating that is easy to stick to, and will keep you feeling stronger, healthier, and more positive about your life all the time.

## I'm Not a Cook, But ...

Let me start this section by telling you I don't cook! Well at least I didn't six years ago when I started getting into shape to compete as a Bikini Diva at the ripe ol' age of sixty-eight. Just a few short years back, my family and especially my husband would have thought my writing a cookbook would have been a cookbook of jokes. Before I started competing, my husband did all the shopping and all the cooking, except for breakfast. Both of us would usually have a veggie or protein shake. That I could handle.

My best friend and competing partner, Babs and I even did a silly cooking video of the way I made spaghetti sauce. We were going to send it into a TV show called *The World's Worst Cooks*. We actually did it as a joke, but what went on in the video turned out to be a joke on us! Smoke was everywhere, and we couldn't stop laughing at my total incompetence in the kitchen. You can see it on my website if you like. And since it was done before we started competing, you can also see the transformation of our bodies, and the way we ate.

About a year into getting my body ready to compete, I started learning about nutrition, and how food gets processed by the body. By the second year, I started preparing foods that would make my body healthier and give me more strength. By the third year, I got really good at knowing what it takes to maintain a strong, healthy, happy body. My husband was generally on board, but sometimes I had to pick and choose from what he would prepare. Lunch was all mine, however, and sometimes I even made dinner. Happily, by the fourth year, with all of the secrets I learned from my fellow competitors, I learned to do meal planning for the week. I even learned how to use seasoning in my food. What a concept! I started experimenting with different meals, and learned to substitute healthier choices for wheat and other carbs that were not contributing to the body I wanted.

Happily, by the fourth year my husband and I were on the same page. We were eating and preparing our food together.

Thinking back to when I started competing, and how I nearly burnt the house down makes me laugh. But now, I experiment with food and desserts all the time, and I'm excited when I find new recipes and ways to cook things. I am blessed to have a husband who, to this day, does the shopping. I'm sure you women out there who have to do it all know how much I appreciate that.

I'm still not a wiz in the kitchen, but I know how to make simple things, and how to make what I prepare look good on a plate. Presentation is very important, especially when you are introducing a new way of eating to your family. Some kids will eat things just because it looks good. I've found when I offer my grandchildren something to eat that looks attractive, they will try it. Then of course it has to taste good to keep their interest. Surprisingly, I've managed to also make it taste good too by using just a few tasty seasonings. I am so excited to share these wonderful recipes and ways of eating that will get you to your goal even quicker.

## Counting or Not Counting Calories

Personally, I don't count calories. When I eat a healthier diet, with the perfect food choices for me, my weight stays pretty much the same.

However, I do gain muscle, and my body gets firmer. If you feel better about counting calories, do it. There are calorie counting books available at almost any bookstore, or charts available online. Following my food charts and exercise regime will get you to your goal for sure. However, for your convenience, I have listed some recipes with calorie totals later in the recipe section of the book to give you an idea of how many calories some foods actually contain.

# More on Eating Clean

I mentioned that I always "eat clean." What that means is that I don't eat processed foods of any kind. My usual rule of thumb is that I only eat one-ingredient foods.

High protein and low carbohydrate foods put your body into a fat burning mode rather than a sugar burning mode. Once into that fat burning mode, the body starts drawing from your fat reserves when it needs energy instead of the sugar and carbohydrate reserves. When you are eating fewer carbohydrates, you will find that you actually have more energy, and don't feel the need to keep eating carbs to supply more energy. In a few words, "Burn fat, not carbs."

Generally speaking, you can eat all the vegetables you like, reasonable portions (four to five ounces) of meat, chicken, fish, eggs, beans, legumes, nuts, and seeds. That's a lot of food to choose from.

# Clean Eating Substitutes

Flour

- Almond flour
- Coconut flour
- Quinoa flour White Rice
- Brown rice

Wild rice

- Quinoa
- Faro
- Barley

- Bulgar
- Spelt Crackers
- Brown rice crackers
- Pecan crackers
- Mary's crackers Tortillas
- Ezekiel sprouted grain tortillas Pizza
- Cauliflower crusts for pizza – Many recipes available online Bread
- Dave's Killer Bread, or other whole grain and seeded bread with no additives

Milk
- Almond milk
- Coconut milk
- Soy milk Margarine
- Coconut oil
- Avocado oil
- Olive oil, extra virgin
- Butter

# Vegan Substitutes (just a few)
Meat, Chicken, Turkey
- Plenty of vegan meat substitutes

Beef or Chicken stock
- Vegetable bouillon cubes Eggs
- Tofu scramble Milk
- Almond, oat, rice, soy, nut, or hemp milk
- Cheese
- Vegan cheeses-*Daiya* makes great vegan cheese

Sour Cream
- Non-dairy yogurt or vegan sour cream Mayonnaise
- Vegan mayonnaise, hummus Honey
- Agave nectar

Now, whether you are vegan or lactose intolerant, you no longer have to give up your favorite "cheesy" foods. Or cheese itself! But be sure to read labels, as some vegetarian cheeses contain casein, which is not vegan. If you can find a great vegan cheese that you like, use it in your recipes in the same manner that you would use dairy cheese.

Don't let this list scare you. I also have some great things to snack on and to curb your sweet tooth that I will share with you later in the book under snacks and desserts.

## Coconut Oil

Coconut oil is classified as a "superfood." Besides using coconut oil in most of my cooking, I also use it on my entire body. The benefits of coconut oil are numerous. They include better brain function, healthier skin, and even weight loss.

Coconut oil has been getting a bad rap from some people because it is a saturated fat. It is actually the healthiest source of saturated fat, and not the kind that you would get from cheese or steak. I could go on and on about the benefits of coconut oil used both exter-nally and internally. I even made my own toothpaste out of it. Just be sure when you put it on your shopping list that you buy organic virgin coconut oil.

## Fiber

If you eat fiber-rich foods, you will not only make your stomach think you're full, you will also be filling up with less calories.

Fiber is a carbohydrate your body can't digest. Most carbs break down and turn to sugar in your system. Fiber won't be broken down into sugar, and passes through the body cleansing as it goes. So, you can see that it helps regulate sugar and blood sugar levels while helping you to feel full.

The best sources of fiber are whole grain foods, fresh fruits and vegetables, legumes, and nuts.

Soluble fiber absorbs water. It helps reduce glucose levels and lowers cholesterol. Some soluble fibers include: beans, lentils, oatmeal, apples, pears, and berries.

Insoluble fiber does not dissolve in water, but is great for moving food through your body. That's great for relieving constipation, and keeping a healthy digestive tract. Insoluble fibers are found in nuts, seeds, legumes, whole grains, brown rice, carrots, tomatoes, cucumbers, celery, broccoli, edamame, brussel sprouts, asparagus, and other veggies.

## Fish

Wild or wild caught fish is always best. They are in their natural state, and contain more natural oils. You will even notice in fish like salmon, that the color of wild salmon is much deeper than farmed salmon. Farmed fish are fed an unnatural diet of genetically modified food and a good dose of antibiotics to keep them from getting sick in the crowded conditions of most farm tanks. Go wild. Eat wild.

## Meat

It's always best to eat grass fed beef and lamb. Again, it's the same principle as eating farmed fish. Most meat is raised on genetically modified foods and antibiotics to keep them from disease and to help them to grow faster. Try to find grass fed or naturally fed meat.

## Chicken and Turkey

Free range naturally fed chicken and turkey is best. A common practice in chicken and turkey farming is to feed them genetically modified food and antibiotics to get them to grow faster. Then, when they are processed, they shoot water into the muscles to "fatten them up" for consumers.

## Eggs

You may not know this, but most eggs are not white. They come in many different colors and speckled patterns. The white eggs you usually buy are bleached to look white. The chickens that lay most of the eggs are kept in small pens and force fed food hormones to keep them laying eggs. Best to buy free range organic eggs. Those chickens usually have a little more room to walk around. They are more expensive however, so use your discretion. I usually buy organic, but sometimes, when I'm not feeling as wealthy, I'll settle for the white eggs.

# Nuts and Seeds

I eat most nuts. For snacking, I eat walnuts, almonds, and pecans, but I also enjoy shelling pistachios. I also occasionally put nuts in my smoothies for an extra burst of protein. Although peanuts are not technically a nut (they are considered legumes), you can also enjoy them like nuts.

I mostly eat sunflower seeds, pumpkin seeds, and squash seeds. There's a lot of nutrition in seeds, so I sprinkle them on salads, or just eat them with some nuts.

# Vegetables

My theory about vegetables is that I can eat all I want of any vegetable except for the starchy ones, which include potatoes and squash. I eat sweet potatoes and yams because they are very high in nutrition, but not white potatoes, and I only eat squash occasionally.

# Potatoes or Yams

Potatoes and sweet potatoes are not the same. Although somewhat similar in their vitamin and mineral content, sweet potatoes and yams are nutritional superstars, and they are far sweeter. White potatoes are starchier, and starch turns to sugar in your bloodstream almost as quickly as eating raw sugar. Sweet potatoes and yams will fill you and keep you satisfied for a longer period of time. Because yams have less starch, you won't get the same "sugar spike" and the resulting "sugar drop" of energy that's on the other side of that spike.

# Beets

If you are really looking for a blast of healthy energy, I suggest you look into beets. I think beets are sweet and delicious, but some people don't like the taste.

If you don't like the taste of beets, but want the benefits they offer, try them in powdered form. Super Beets makes a great powdered beet supplement that you can mix with water. They also have black cherry flavored powdered beets. I take a teaspoon of Super Beets powder with four ounces of water just before I leave the house for a workout at the gym, and within a few minutes, I feel a powerful surge of energy that supercharges my workouts. That surge of energy is the result of an increase in nitric oxide that beets gives me.

In the 1980's, three scientists won the Nobel Prize for discovering the importance of nitric oxide in the body. This miracle molecule oxygenates the blood, and is made naturally in the body when you are younger. As you age it lessens. Taking just one spoonful of Super Beets brings that energy right back to my body. Try it.

# Fruits

Fruits are filled with antioxidants that help firm up your skin, delay wrinkles and discoloration, nourish your skin, and keep you youthful. But beware! Fruits are also filled with fructose, which is a form of sugar.

That's why they taste so yummy, but it's also why we should eat them sparingly. Adding a lot of sugar to your diet, even in the form of fructose from fruit, works against effective weight loss, and keeps your body in the sugar burning mode rather than the more effective fat burning mode.

Berries are filled with antioxidants, and are relatively low in fructose. I add them to my salads and smoothies or eat a few for dessert.

Apples are also great as a light snack because, besides their nutritional benefits, they are loaded with fiber. I cut up apples and add a little almond butter as a special treat occasionally.

# Drinks
## The Value of Water
If you don't already drink plenty of water, plain or with lemon, start. Besides helping to curb your appetite, it flushes impurities from your system, and hydrates your skin. You can also infuse your water with mint, cucumber, and almost anything that suits your fancy. There are even portable water bottles with the infusers built right in. Just add your own flavors.

## Hot Tea After Meals
For the best results in weight loss, drink a cup of hot tea after each meal. Preferably green or peppermint tea. It will help you digest your meal quicker, and would be a very healthy choice for any diet. For other times, iced tea is a cool choice to make. But no sugar.

## Bubbly Drinks
I am a big fan of the bubbly. When I first started getting into shape not a day went by without a Pepsi or two. I

thought nothing of downing a Dr. Brown's Black Cherry Cola, or Cel-Ray tonic with my meal. I actually thought it was a big thing in my first year of changing my body that I switched from Pepsi to Diet Pepsi! I have to admit I loved the taste of all the sodas. But, when I did the research and found out the diseases and illnesses that were attached to the sugar and chemicals contained in those drinks, I forced myself to switch to more healthful drinks.

At first I was miserable and craved my daily Pepsis. But then I created some affirmations for myself, and I got busy building a new belief about soda. I bought a Soda Stream soda-making machine. They are readily available these days in most department stores. If you don't want to buy a machine, you can just buy bottled soda water, and start mixing it with natural juices you squeeze yourself. I would squeeze lemons, limes, even cucumbers and celery juice. You can filter out the pulp if it bothers you by pouring the juice through a cheese cloth, paper towel, or fine strainer.

With that change, and getting used to drinking unsweetened iced tea, I lost the taste for sugar based sodas with all their chemicals and toxins, and enjoyed drinking my healthy bubbly.

## Coffee vs Gano

Coffee is acceptable, but it is acidic. Learn to drink your coffee with limited amounts of milk or cream, and definitely no sugar. If you are a coffee drinker, let me suggest a substitute. *Gano* is one of my favorite products. It's a nutritious healthful beverage made from coffee that has been infused with Ganoderma Lucidum, a special mushroom extract that is the world's most alkaline rich product. *Gano* changes the acid in coffee into alkaline, which makes this coffee the healthiest gift for your body.

Plus, it's delicious. I drink a cup every morning before my shake. And on a hot day, it's great with ice. Go to my website under products and try some for yourself.

## Meal Prepping

When the lunch and dinner meals are prepared ahead of time, it is easier to stay on the diet. What you don't want is to be caught hungry without good healthy food around. Eating lots of smaller healthy snacks during the day is a great way to keep from getting hungry and bingeing on a lot of unhealthy food. Meal planning is a great way to avoid the bingeing, and make sure that you always have healthy alternatives at hand.

The easiest way for me to plan my meals is to take some time on a Sunday afternoon or evening and prepare enough food for the next three days.

Sometimes, I prepare for the entire week, depending on what I'm eating that week. For example, If I know I'm going to be eating a lot of salmon that week, I'll cut it into meal-sized portions, and cook up three or four days worth. I always undercook my meat and fish a little so that it still stays moist when I heat it up later. Often, I will make the meat or fish just before I actually eat it, but I always make enough veggies for the entire week so I can grab some anytime I want.

Again, I undercook them just a bit so they stay tasty after reheating.

If you are thinking that this sounds like a lot of work, trust me, as a person who hardly set foot in the kitchen before I got serious about getting into shape, you can do it! It takes about the same amount of time as preparing a regular meal, but you're just cooking larger amounts.

If meal prepping is your challenge, it's time for an affirmation.

*I have plenty of time for my new diet and for my new lifestyle.*

Or

*I know the choices I am making now are the reason I will reach my goal!*

Before you know it, meal prepping will become a habit, and you will look forward to knowing your food is always there for you when you need it. A little preparation goes a long way.

---

**TIP**
**Invest in really good Tupperware or other airtight plastic containers. I have some I bought at Costco that have tops with rubber gaskets and snap lock seals. They work so well that I've kept food fresh for up to two weeks.**

---

---

**Tip**
Make sure you always have healthy snacks in
your fridge or pantry to grab when you feel
hungry or need to satisfy some emotional urge.

---

## Snacks

If you're a crunch person, find some healthy crunchy foods like celery, peppers, or green beans you can eat raw or dip into some hummus or tahini.

If you're a sweets person, keep a banana or some other fruits around. You don't want to go nuts on fruit either, but it's better than sugar or sugar substitutes.

If you're a salty snack person, try celery, which has a good salty taste, or take just a few quinoa chips, or any of the chips listed in the substitute list. But try to give up the urge to eat too many salty foods. Salt adds to water retention and can give you that "puffy" look.

## TIPS TO FOOL YOUR MIND

If you really want to get control over what is going into your body, then you will need to change your thinking about both the kind of food, and the amount of food you put into it. Americans eat way too much food. Our restaurants dole out more than any reasonable stomach can hold, let alone digest properly. Supersize meals with fries on the side have become the norm instead of the exception.

---

**TIP**
**Smaller Meals Satisfy**

---

Remembering that the mind is a powerful muscle, you can actually build that muscle to be satisfied with less food.

---

**TIP**
**Use Smaller Plates**

---

One of the little tricks that I love sharing with everyone is so simple, and it really works. When you serve yourself food, use smaller plates. We use salad plates. They are about half the size of a normal dinner plate.

You can still fill your smaller plate but resist the temptation to stack food on your plate. Just take enough to fill the plate. That will be enough for your body to be properly nourished. Your mind translates a full plate into a full meal, and you will be satisfied with less. In no time, you will get used to eating less. It's just that simple.

If you really want to lock this idea into your consciousness and strengthen that mind-muscle, use an affirmation along with it. You could say:

*My stomach is completely satisfied with this meal.*

Or

*The amount of food I'm eating nourishes me completely.*

---

**TIP**

**Cut your veggies into smaller pieces to make it look like there's more on your plate and chew your food completely.**

---

Just like with the use of smaller plates, you can fool your mind into thinking you are consuming more food by eating many more pieces of food. You can also add to that habit by chewing your food completely before swallowing.

The feeling of being full is not caused by filling your stomach. It is actually a chemical reaction. The food and drink hits your stomach, and mixes with the digestive juices. It takes your brain about twenty minutes to register the reaction. If you eat slower and chew your food completely, it gives the brain a chance to catch up to the chemical process happening in your stomach and sends you the message that you're full before you've eaten too much. Those chemicals continue to develop even after your meal for about half an hour, and the chemical levels in your blood stay elevated for up to five hours. It's only when those levels begin to drop that you start feeling hungry again. If you were to measure your levels often, like most diabetics, you would know that it takes quite a while for your blood sugar levels to drop after a meal.

When I first started cutting down on the volume of food I was taking in, I used to take four or five carrots for my snack and dip them in hummus. Or occasionally, I'd take a huge apple, cut it into pieces and spread almond butter on each piece. I also chewed my food quickly but not completely, and often swallowed without breaking down the food in my mouth first. The result was that even after eating all the carrots or all the apple, I always wanted more. When the idea of using smaller plates sunk in, I thought about taking smaller snacks as well. So, what I did was to cut one carrot in quarters lengthwise, then cut that into small sections, so that I could fill the plate with carrot sections and feel like I was eating more. I also sliced only half the apple into thin slices and put even less almond butter on those slices. Then I chewed all my food completely before swallowing, which allowed me to savor the food more completely. I was totally satisfied because it felt like I was eating more, but in fact I was eating less.

# Chapter 5:
# Recipes

Below are typical recipes for breakfast, lunch, dinner, and snacks that will give you an idea of how to eat. Pick what you want, or make up your own variations, using low carb foods you prefer.

## BREAKFAST
### Saba's Morning Shake
Protein powder-one scoop (I prefer chocolate, but choose your flavor)

1 banana

¼ cup of blueberries

5 or 6 almonds or walnuts

1 cup water or ½ cup water and ½ cup almond milk
Add ice to preference.

Blend until smooth.

About the Ingredients:

Almonds: Besides protein and oils, they contain Vitamin E for healthy skin and eyes.

Walnuts: High in protein, oil, and antioxidants.

Blueberries: Also high in antioxidants and other nutrients, and low in calories. They are also best for warding off heart disease, protecting against DNA damage, and fighting off cancer. Blueberries lead the pack in anti-aging benefits.

Bananas: There are so many reasons to eat bananas:

They are a natural mood enhancer.

They help prevent kidney cancer.

They protect the eyes against macular degeneration.
They build strong bones.

Even the peel can be used to remove warts and shine your shoes. (Really. You can Google it.)

Oh yes, and they are delicious.

## My Husband's Veggie Smoothie

Best if blended with a Vitamix or Blendtec blender. These powerful blenders will help emulsify even the most difficult veggies or roots.

Add to taste …

Any green leafy vegetable or herb:

Kale, spinach, mustard greens, collard greens, cabbage, cilantro,parsley, etc.

Berries:

Blueberries, strawberries, raspberries

Avocado or banana to thicken, or a tablespoon of olive oil

Be creative.

Add red or green peppers, broccoli, green beans, celery, ginger, or any other veggie.

Ice

Blend until smooth.

Soon you'll be creating your own inventions and find the perfect blend for you.

# LUNCH
## Saba's Hearty Salad

My favorite is a hearty salad along with some avocado, cucumbers, and tomatoes.

Mix:

Your favorite greens.

> If you substitute spinach or kale for lettuce it will be a much healthier meal for you. Or maybe a mix of greens would suit you better. There are many pre-mixed blends of greens in most grocery stores, or you can mix them yourself.

For protein, you can add chicken, shrimp, or a hard-boiled egg.

Add fruit:

> If you want to add more excitement, add a few berries (strawberries, blueberries, raspberries, or blackberries), pomegranate seeds, a piece of cut-up apple, or ¼ banana.

---

**TIP**
**The danger with salads is not the salad itself, but what kind of and how much dressing you use. A simple oil and vinegar dressing or some salsa is perfect, but if you really feel the need for a creamy rich dressing, then just use a teaspoon and mix it in well.**

---

# Sandwiches and Wraps

I often use up leftovers for my sandwiches. You can really get creative with your choices.

There are many good healthy breads out there these days. I prefer Dave's Killer Bread, or Ezekiel 4:9 Sprouted Whole Grain Bread because they both use minimal amounts of flour.

If you use bread, get used to eating open-faced sandwiches, or make a half sandwich and cut it in two to look like a full sandwich on a small plate.

If you prefer a wrap, you can use healthy sprouted grain tortillas (Ezekiel 4:9 tortillas are great) or you can use whole grain tortillas to wrap your food. You can also wrap your food in seaweed for an added Asian flavor.

You can use avocado and tomato to make it moist and eliminate the need for mayonnaise. Small amounts of mustard or horseradish are okay as well.

Sprinkle some sprouts, nuts, or seeds to add crunch.

# Snacks

Here is a list of healthy things you can snack on that I like:

- Carrots and hummus
- Celery and almond butter or peanut butter (plain and natural, without sugar or other additives)
- Pumpkin, sunflower or squash seeds
- Unsalted peanuts and pistachio nuts in the shell
- Walnuts or almonds–preferably unsalted
- Any fruit from my list of acceptable fruits

# RECIPES WITH A CALORIE COUNT

I know we talked about counting calories before, so for those of you who want to count, I put them in each recipe to make it easier for you. These are just a few of my recipes to give you an idea of how to count calories. There are many books out there with calorie counts. Get creative with your choices and have fun.

---

**TIP**
**A typical serving is usually about 4 ounces.**
**A good rule of thumb to use is, if it's bigger**
**than the size of your palm, it's too big.**

---

## Mock Taco Salad

Choose your protein:

> Chicken (1/4 of a serving, 36 calories)
> White fish (1/3 of a serving, 21 calories)
> Beef (85 calories)

½ medium avocado (125 calories)

2 tablespoons of Organic Jack's Cantina Style Salsa (10 calories) 1/4 cup of Trader Joe's Cuban Style Black Beans (50 Calories)

7 veggie or flaxseed tortilla chips (7 chips equal 130 calories)

> If you must have chips, look for some of the healthier chips that are out there now. There are a few out there made from lentils or quinoa instead of corn and wheat or potato.

Mash the avocado with 2 tablespoons of Organic Jack's Cantina Style Salsa.

Add 1/4 cup of black beans.

Surround this wonderful Mexican delight with a few chips and there you have a great lunch.

Add it all together and this healthy meal comes to anywhere from 336 – 400 calories, depending on what protein you choose to put in it.

You can also exchange vegetarian ingredients. Either way it's yummy and filling.

## Burrito

The burrito is the same ingredients as the taco salad, only you can use an Ezekiel tortilla (look these up on our food list) to roll it up. And because I like crunchy, I add two tortilla chips inside before I roll it up. The tortilla is 150 calories, but I only use half, so it comes in at only 75 calories.

## Stir-Fry Lunch

As a base, choose from quinoa, faro, or brown rice.

½ cup of quinoa, (120 calories)

½ cup faro, (50 calories)

½ cup brown rice (108 calories)

½ cup of shrimp (36 calories)

1 cup sugar snap pea pods (17 calories)

1 thin slice of green, red, or yellow pepper (2 or 3 calories)

½ scallion (2 or 3 calories)

First chop the pepper and scallion. Then sauté the shrimp, pea pods, pepper, and onion together, and season to taste. When the sauté is done, place on top of your choice of grain. This can be a nice hot lunch or even your dinner. This light delightful meal adds up to 109 – 179 calories depending on your choice of grain.

# Vegan

1 medium-sized beet, cooked (37 calories) 1 small corn on the cob (100 calories)

1 cup of sugar snap peas (17 calories) 1 cup cooked spinach (23 calories)

If you're in the mood for a light lunch this will hit the spot for you. Just place the beets, corn on the cob, spinach, and the sugar snap peas on a small plate, and you have a tasty and filling lunch that comes in at 177 calories.

# Veggie Plate

You can always go light for lunch. Slice up some cucumbers, red or green peppers, carrots, broccoli, or any other veggies. Arrange them in a colorful pattern on your plate. Remember, half the job is to make it look really delicious. Veggies, as a rule, are always very low in calories.

## Sweet Kale Salad Mix

We often eat a nice sweet kale salad packaged to perfection by Eat Smart costing $4.95 a bag, which lasts the entire week and is only 80 calories per serving.

If you're not vegan you can add a hard-boiled egg.

In a big hurry? You can take the same ingredients as above and roll it up in seaweed. And one sheet of seaweed is only 5 calories.

## Make Your Own Sushi

¼ cup or 1 ounce of crabmeat (27 calories) or shrimp (18 calories)

½ hard-boiled egg (39 calories)

1 inch of cucumber cut into thin strips (about 6 calories)

1 sheet of seaweed (5 calories)

Cut the shrimp or crabmeat into pieces.

Mash the hard-boiled egg so it has a creamy consistency. Mix the two ingredients together.

Season to taste.

Slice the cucumber into very thin pieces, almost spaghetti-like. Place the seaweed sheet on a plate and dampen the ends of the seaweed so it will stick together.

Spoon the mixture onto the seaweed ½ inch from the end of the sheet. Place the cucumber strips on the top of your mixture and roll it up. Seal the seaweed with moisture.

All together this light lunch adds up to only 68 calories, 77 if you use crab. You could even have two! If you decide to make two remember one whole egg is 78 calories.

When I first decided to make my own sushi, it looked far from professional. Kind of sloppy actually. I served it to my family and it opened up before they could get the first bite in. It took practice, but now I'm a wiz at it. So, don't give up if your first one or first few don't look like your local sushi bar's. Just as your mind-body connection takes time, so does rolling sushi. But it's so worth it in the end.

## A Cold Plate

1 hard-boiled egg (78 calories)

½ cup baby tomatoes (14 calories)

¼ cup crabmeat (27 calories)

¼ cup shrimp (18 calories)

1/2 medium avocado (125 calories)

1 cup sugar snap pea pods (17 calories) 1 cup raw spinach (7 calories)

See how creative you can be with this list of things to munch on. A delicious and filling idea is to take a hard-boiled egg and cut it in half. Then take a couple of baby tomatoes and chop them up. Mix the two ingredients together, add a rounded teaspoon of cut up crabmeat or shrimp, and place this combination into half of the avocado. Squeeze a little lemon on top for flavor and enjoy.

---

**TIP**

**Usually the urge to eat something comes when you are not busy. So, get busy doing something creative, or even routine, and see if you lose the urge to stuff your face. Just Do It. Also, try journaling or writing new affirmations.**

---

## DESSERT RECIPES
### Chocolate

For those of you who just can't stay away from chocolate, I have a wonderful treat. Although I am not a chocoholic, when I started getting healthy and fit, I still craved the taste of chocolate. So, I figured out a way to still get my chocolate fix and keep it healthy at the same time.

I tried a lot of protein bars looking for one or two that were tasty without adding much sugar or sweetener to my diet. I will recommend two bars, Zone Bars and Think Thin Bars. They come in different flavors, and I love them all. You can get them at almost any drug store or grocery store for around less than two dollars per bar, and even cheaper on Amazon. At Costco, you can buy twenty-four bars for a great price at below a dollar each.

At first, I would eat a bar in the middle of the afternoon, but then I came up with this idea on how to satisfy my desire for chocolate, and not only lower the calorie intake, but control my chocolate cravings.

## Saba's Low-Cal Candy Fake Out

Here's what to do:

Take 3 flavors of Zone bars, or your favorite flavors of Think Thin bars. Each bar is about 210 calories, which equals the same calories as 4 pieces of a regular box of See's candy.

Cut the bars into small pieces (maybe ½ inch squares) so they appear to be actual pieces of chocolate candy that you would get in a regular box from a candy store.

Place them in an old empty box of candy, or go to a box store and get a nice little thin box to put the pieces in. Make it look really nice with some tissue paper or fancy little cups to hold the pieces. You can even have fun designing a new cover for the box with your name on it. The more you make it look like a delicious box of candy, the more you'll enjoy it.

---

**TIP**
**When you put the candy in a nice box you are fooling your mind again, just as you did by using smaller plates. But you'd better not eat more than three pieces.**

---

Remember you're still consuming calories you don't really need. So, take it easy. This is merely a way of indulging a habit that will diminish if you do not give into it. This trick worked for me, and I know it will work for you.

Here are some affirmations you can say to yourself that will help you change your thinking about what you are doing in a positive way:

*This candy is delicious and satisfying.*

*I am eating chocolate and still losing weight.*

*This chocolate candy is good for me, and I can have a couple of pieces guilt free.*

AND here's something to think about if you are a calorie counter:

Two pieces of candy in a regular box of candy is usually anywhere from 160 – 180 calories. Your average box of candy (about 20 pieces) adds up to 1600 – 1800 calories. Saba's Fake Out Candy is also 20 pieces but adds up to only 630 calories! That comes to about 32 calories apiece. At that rate, you could eat the whole box. But don't! I created this to help satisfy your sweet tooth and lead you away from sugar.

Here are some affirmations that go along with Saba's Fake Out candy:

*I am happy to be changing the way I eat sweets.*

*This is a great way to be satisfied as I cut sugar out of my diet.*

## Saba's Sweet & Delish Mock Candy (for diabetics)

You'll need: A frying pan Coconut oil

2 eggs

½ cup of your choice of berries – Strawberries in season are the sweetest, but you can use blackberries, blueberries or any other berries you like.

½ cup crushed almonds or pecans

½ tsp stevia

½ tsp vanilla for flavoring

Beat the eggs with a whisk or fork.

Add the stevia and/or vanilla and whisk again until blended.

Slice your strawberries thin and keep them handy. If you are using other berries, cut them in half.

Heat your frying pan on a high flame, then reduce to medium. Lightly grease your frying pan with coconut oil or spray.

Pour the egg mixture into the pan and let it get slightly cooked (about halfway cooked).

Add almonds or pecans and your fruit choice. Fold it in half like an omelet.

Cover the pan, and let it sit for a few minutes.

Turn the omelet and replace the cover for a minute or so. Remove it from the pan and place it on a plate.

Put it in the freezer, and let it cool for fifteen or twenty minutes.

Take it out of the freezer and cut the omelet into small candy sized pieces.

Place the squares on waxed paper inside a small box or even an old candy box. (You can layer the pieces between wax paper if you like.)

Store the box in the freezer.

You can take out one or two pieces when you have the urge to have a piece of candy. Just let it thaw out for about ten or fifteen minutes, and you have a sugar free, healthy piece of candy that won't put any weight on you at all. Feel free to experiment with your ingredients. Have fun with this one.

After I created this sugarless treat, I put the video of how to make it on my website. It was so heartwarming when I got a post from a ten-year-old girl who had diabetes and craved candy. She said she felt left out when everyone around her was eating candy and she couldn't have any. She tried my recipe, and to her amazement she loved it, and thanked me for changing her life. Now she was able to enjoy something sweet and sugar free.

# Guilt-Free Popsicles

When I was a kid, my family would always finish dinner and sit around together to watch television while we ate ice cream. I loved ice cream. But getting healthy led me to make the choice of giving up dairy products of all kinds. You would be surprised at how dairy puts weight on you. But loving that creamy taste forced me to create my own rich and delicious dairy free popsicle.

When you make your popsicles taste good, your mind thinks popsicles are like ice cream, and you won't feel deprived at all. Along with the great taste, the affirmations are training your mind to be satisfied with a healthy alternative. So, here are some suggestions of what you can use to make these tasty frozen treats.

First, go out and buy two or three sets of plastic popsicle containers. They're available at Target, Ikea, and many other stores. You will also need a blender to put your ingredients together.

Depending on what consistency you like, you can blend things together for your own desired thickness. In the summer, you can use all kinds of fruits to make "fruit-sicles." They come out sweet without the addition of any kind of sweetener.

Here are some ingredients you can play around with:

Almond milk

Bananas Fruit Nuts

Protein powder (choose your flavor) Stevia powder, if needed.

Depending on how many you're making, blend the ingredients you think would taste the best until they come to a loose paste consistency. This will help suspend some of the fruit pulp and seeds so they won't all drop to the bottom of the popsicle. I prefer the pulp and particles, but if you prefer, you can take a sieve or strainer to filter them out.

I did a lot of experimenting to get the blend of ingredients to a thickness that resembled melted ice cream before freezing it. If you want the

consistency of popsicles, add more liquid. They are both delicious. Try them both and see what you like best.

After you blend your mixture together, pour it into the popsicle containers, and place them in the freezer. Leave a little room at the top for expansion while freezing. If you have kids, this is a perfect way to get them used to eating delicious treats without them knowing it's healthy and contains no added sugar.

This might even peak your family's interest in hearing more about the way you are changing the way you eat. But don't mention that there is no sugar before they even try the treats. What they don't know won't hurt them.

Here are some affirmations that will help you with this:

*I know everyone around me can see the difference in my body and my attitude.*

*What I am doing for myself will have a good effect on others around me.*

*As I get healthier, thinner, and stronger, it is easier to share my experience.*

*Through my choices, I am becoming an inspiration to others.*

These are just a few yummy desserts to get you started. Don't be afraid to be creative and come up with your own now that you know ingredients that not only won't affect your dieting but will help you on the road to perfect health.

# CHAPTER 6:
# A DAY IN THE LIFE OF
# THINK IT, DO IT, BE IT

Now let's put the Think It, Do It, Be It method into practice while you use it to go through a day in your life.

What follows are many of the activities that take place during a typical day in the life of an average working person, and how to incorporate the Think It, Do It, Be It method into your life. If you do not leave your house for a job, or if you are a stay at home mom, dad, student, or retired this will be easy for you to follow too. Although it may seem like a lot to remember at first, stay with it. Like anything else in life, practice makes perfect. I have also given you a checklist at the end of this section so you can chart your progress. I've also included a weekly checklist at the end of the book with all the other charts and diets for easy reference. For most people, it takes twenty-one days to change a habit. I suggest that you make at least three copies of the weekly checklist so that you have twenty-one days to check off, plus extra days if you need them.

Remember to have fun with this and enjoy the process of building a new habit.

## Morning

Before getting out of bed, take a few deep breaths. Fill your lungs with oxygen, the energy of life.

Consciously give thanks for everything in your life. Start listing things that you love and for which you are grateful. The list can be as long as you like, as long as it's positive thoughts about life.

Starting with positive thoughts gives you untold amounts of energy and will enable you to go about your day feeling great right from the start. All your thoughts attract energy. Do you want "I'm tired and grumpy" energy, or would you rather have "I see the beauty of life" energy?

---

**TIP**
**Whatever you are grateful for**
**always increases in your life**.

---

An easy way to start off your day being grateful is to give thanks for the simple fact that you woke up to life today. Not just that you're alive, but that you see life in a whole new perspective. You are doing something positive with your life today, and taking steps toward achieving long sought goals. Being grateful to be alive, and affirming that your day will be productive, will attract everything you need to move you forward on your journey.

Then, lovingly give up control for the day. As the saying goes, "The best laid plans of mice and men often go awry." It's how flexible we are in dealing with those surprises that ensures our success.

Understand that a thing, or an event, simply is what it is. It is up to you to make it either work or not work in your life. How you focus your energy dictates how your life flows. Think about that when things come up or challenge you during your day.

## Set the Mood

The next step is to set the mood for your day. Never let the weather get you down. That is easy for someone to say who lives in sunny Southern California, where the warmth of the sun can be such a regenerative force. But weather changes everywhere. It does what it does. It's how you react to it that makes your day work.

In California, it often rains for long periods of time in the winter. The weather can be quite chilling too, not freezing zero-degree weather, but chilling nevertheless. I used to let the weather get to me. Cold for me is anything below sixty degrees. I like it sunny and hot. When it got cold, I would feel down, sometimes listless, and uninspired. My husband is just the opposite. He says he comes alive in cooler weather. Everyone's different, but everyone can make the best of whatever conditions they encounter.

In colder weather, it would often take a big push just to get myself to the gym. And even a bigger push to have an attitude that allowed me to be energetic and happy. After I created the Think It, Do It, Be It method, I not only changed my body, I changed my whole life, and even how I think about the weather. Now it's time for you to take control of how you choose to live your life. If I could make drastic changes in my life and my routines at sixty-eight years of age, you can do it at your age.

Bottom line, take the time to set your mood for the day. It makes a big difference and makes you a more pleasant person.

## Stretch

After you're up, stretch out your muscles. Send your body the message that it's going to be used today, and you want it to be ready and receptive.

## The Calf Stretch

While brushing your teeth and hair, rise up and down a few times on your toes. It's a great way to stretch and firm your feet, calves, and ankles.

## The Long Stretch

When you put your pants on, or if you wear a dress then do this when you put your panties on, do a complete bend from the waist, and put your hands on the ground. Step into your pants or panties and pull them up.

But don't stop there. After your pants or panties are on, continue the movement up with your arms, and stretch them up as high as you can as you tighten your buttocks, and bend back slightly. Aah, feels great to stretch, doesn't it? Now touch the ground again and repeat the long stretch. Hint: Make sure your pants or panties are firmly secured first. Ha ha.

# Now It's Time for Breakfast

What you put into your body really affects how efficiently your body functions, and how effectively you use your energy to get into shape. Just downing a cup of coffee or eating a toaster pop-up isn't helping you get healthy or stay in shape.

Who doesn't like the smell of fresh brewed coffee? But it can be too acidic for some folks. Try to be aware of how the acid of coffee affects your body. I mentioned earlier that a fantastic alternative is a product that tastes a lot like coffee but is completely alkaline. It's called Gano, and it is a favorite find for those of us who are sensitive to acidic foods and drinks.

If you prefer tea, go ahead.

Probably the most effective way to start your metabolism burning right away is to have a little lemon in hot water. You'll get an instant buzz, and your body will get the message that it's time to start burning calories.

Oatmeal is a good choice but see if you can eat it without sugar. Cutting up part of an apple or adding some berries and nuts can be a great way to replace the desire for sugar.

If you're not the oatmeal type, you might try a healthy shake. Look in the recipe section of this book for a great shake recipe.

As the mixture is blending, or if you decided on oatmeal, do this exercise while it's cooking:

## The Counter/Chair Stretch

Put your leg up on the counter or on the seat of a chair if a counter is too difficult. Grab your toes or whatever you can grab and try to lay your chest on your leg. Just do what you can and let yourself relax into the stretch. Then switch legs.

As you drink your shake or eat your oatmeal, think about being grateful for the opportunity to work exercise into your day, and for how good your food tastes. Keep the gratitude train rolling.

Here is a perfect place to use one of your affirmations.

*I am grateful that I stretch with ease as I get closer to my goal.*

---

**TIP**
**Affirming what you desire builds the mental strength you need to fulfill your desires.**

---

See how easy this is? You woke up, gave thanks, brushed your teeth, brushed your hair, prepared and ate your breakfast, stimulated your mind, and stretched your body. You should feel different, more positive and happier in general. Pay attention to that feeling. Wallow in it. Give thanks for it.

## Your Workout

As you have seen, you can incorporate exercise into almost anything you do during your day. But it helps to have a more regular workout scheduled in your day where that is all you're doing. Whether you go to a gym or use your own exercise equipment at home, make it a habit to work out daily. It can come at any time you choose but be sure to fit it into your day at some time. I remember hearing from my step-daughter that, on some days, she would ride her stationary bike for half an hour before going to bed because she promised herself that she would exercise every day, and she was too busy to exercise earlier. That's dedication. And if you really want to change your body and your life, you must dedicate yourself to developing new habits that include exercise. You can go to the gym and develop your own routines or watch one of my videos at home. But be sure to get your workout in before going to bed.

## On Your Way to Work
Make every activity a chance to exercise.

## Lunges
With each step, bend your forward knee deeply, and almost touch your back knee to the ground. Your front knee should be bent without extending it past your front foot. Then switch as you make your way to the car. It might look a little weird, but you and your butt will be happy you did it.

---

### TIP

**Do a few lunges around the house as you are picking up your things to take with you for the day.**

---

## Door Stretch

If you drive to work, before you even get into the car, open the door and put your hands on the top of the rim of your car door opening. Push your arms straight out, step your feet back two or three feet and lean forward keeping your arms straight and pulling the muscles of your thighs up. You should feel it in your thighs, shoulders, neck, lower back, and chest. Hold that stretch for at least thirty seconds.

---

**TIP**
**You can also do this stretch at home by grabbing the top or the sides of any door frame and leaning forward.**

---

## Neck and Wrist Rolls

At stop lights or traffic jams, alternate circling your head to the left and to the right. And/or make a fist and circle your hands with inside turns, and then outside turns.

## Breathing

We usually don't give our breath much thought, but breathing is a wonderful fitness exercise. It not only keeps you alive, but also, if done in a conscious manner, stimulates your brain, calms you down, feeds oxygen to the muscles and keeps you in the present moment. So, take a minute and try something called the fire breath.

## The Fire Breath

Right after you park your car, close your eyes, and with your eyes closed, look up towards your third eye – that spot between your eyebrows. Pay special attention to forcing your breath out quickly through your nose with every exhale. Notice your abdomen sucking up and in as you force each breath out. Try to get in about a breath a second for one minute. If that's too much for you, just do what you can for a minute. This will stimulate your brain and clear your head. By the time you get to work, you should be relaxed, energized, and ready to take on the day.

## Break Time

At your break time, if you are one of the lucky ones who don't crave sugar, try to bring things from home for your snacks like celery and almond butter, or carrots and hummus. I love to munch on pumpkin seeds, but sunflower seeds are also great. I get them in the shell, so that I don't just grab a handful of seeds and start chewing them. I work for my seeds. Besides being more fun, shelling them yourself slows you down so you eat less, and allows you to digest better. If you're craving something sweet, I suggest eating a protein bar. Zone Bars, Think Thin, and Quest are my favorites. Look for some that are low in calories and very low in sugar.

---

**TIP**
**Remember to drink at least eight ounces of water with your snack to hydrate and to help give you a feeling of being full.**

---

Before going back to work sit quietly for a moment, and repeat this affirmation:

> *I am doing everything necessary for a healthier and stronger body. I love how I feel, and I love how I look.*

Repeat it a few times. Say it every day until you believe it. You'll be pleasantly surprised at how well it works.

The mind needs constant affirmation to adopt a new attitude and belief. Just think how long it took you to develop some of your negative beliefs about your body. Don't you think it's about time to put some good thoughts in there to counter all the false negative thoughts you've allowed yourself to believe over the years? Affirmations work. Use them.

## After Your Break

When you go back to your desk try this:

## Stand Ups

Sit on the edge of your chair. Straighten your back and stand up keeping your back as straight as possible. Do that ten times. If this is too hard for you, do three or five of these until you can work up to ten.

So, you've strengthened your mind, had your snack, and worked out your legs and glutes, energized yourself, and it's only mid-morning!

Before you go on to lunch, take a quick look at the picture of your desired body that you kept handy to inspire yourself.

Now would be a good time to give yourself another positive affirmation:

*I am excited about taking action towards being fit.*

## Lunchtime

Do yourself a favor and have a sensible lunch. If your choice is a salad, flash it up. Maybe make it more filling by adding chicken or shrimp, or some avocado or a hard-boiled egg. Look at the lunch recipes in the recipe section of this book.

A simple oil and vinegar dressing is perfect, but if you really feel the need for a creamy rich dressing, then just use a teaspoon full, and mix it with a little water to thin it out. This might take some getting used to, but it will make it a lot easier if you practice. As you eat, you can strengthen your BS (Belief System) by affirming,

*This choice is helping me reach my goal with ease.*

**Or**

*My craving for unhealthy things is diminishing. I am grateful for that.*

---

**TIP**
**Remember: The danger with salads is not the salad itself, but in what kind and how much dressing you use.**

---

## Healthy Burgers

If you have the kind of job that allows you to go out for lunch, and you crave burgers and fries, get the burger, but without the bread. Most restaurants know about "the wrap" where they wrap your burger in lettuce to take the place of bread. Replace the fries with lettuce and tomatoes, or a small salad.

If you have that feeling that you are practically starving before lunch, I suggest you get into the practice of drinking at least eight ounces of water just before your lunch break. If your hunger cravings are nagging at you after you're done with your lunch, drink another glass of water or some tea, and repeat these affirmations to yourself:

*I am satisfied with what I'm feeding my body. The rewards are feeling healthy and fit.*

*Every day it gets easier and easier.*

The trick is to say it until you believe it. So, say it with a smile, and know it's working for you.

## After Lunch Walk or Climb

After your lunch take a brisk walk around the block if you can. If you're stuck inside, walk around hallways or as much as you can wherever you are. If you have a staircase where you work, even better!

If you are a beginner, walk up and down the staircase as much as you can without pushing yourself. Do this a few times. You will find yourself getting stronger and able to do more day by day. Soon, you'll be running up and down the stairs.

## Afternoon Break

We've already discussed what kind of break-time food to eat. If you're like me, you might feel like you really need some kind of an energy pick-up mid-afternoon. I suggest you try a cup of Gano or green tea, or possibly some warm water with lemon again. But try to stay away from blended sweetened coffee drinks and sugar treats. They give you a temporary boost, but then they slam you down again leaving you with no energy, and a big temptation to eat some junk food to keep you going.

Now, let me tell you what you can do to tighten your stomach and strengthen your arms during your break or anytime you can fit it in.

## The Tummy Tightener

Sit on your chair and place your hands on the tops of your knees keeping your arms straight. Curl your back into a C shape, and while you push down with your arms, raise your heels and push up your legs up as you tighten your stomach. You're pushing down with your arms, tightening your stomach, and pushing up with your legs. Do this fifty to one hundred times for a few seconds each.

If someone asks what you're doing, just say you're saving thousands of dollars on a tummy tuck. Or turn them on to my book.

# The Drive Home

On your drive home, when your car is at a complete stop, you can do a couple of my *Autosize* exercises.

# The Steering Wheel Squeeze

Grab the outside of your steering wheel with your hands, bend your elbows out, and press in and squeeze the steering wheel for as many times as you can until you're ready to drive again.

Next time you stop your car, do the same thing with your arms, only this time keep your arms straight while squeezing the wheel with your forearms. By the time you get home, you'll be amazed at how much you have strengthened your chest and your arms.

If you are on a bus, train, or in a cab just put your hands together in prayer position and lower your arms so that they are chest level. Now turn your right hand into a fist shape and push it against your left hand as you resist the push. Do this ten times, and then switch hands, turning your left hand into a fist and repeating the same action. Do this as many times as you can until it's easy to do one hundred on each side.

**WARNING:
NEVER DO ANY OF THESE EXERCISES WHILE THE CAR IS MOVING. YOU NEED TO KEEP YOUR MIND ON YOUR DRIVING**.

Spend your time in the car wisely. Later in this book you will learn how to do a complete workout in your car with

*Saba's Autosize.* I have also included pictures of the above exercises and more in that section.

# Dinner

The best thing that you can do for yourself at dinner is to stop just before you eat and affirm:

> *Thank you for this healthy food. I know that it is helping me create the healthy body I desire.*

Then picture that body in your mind and relish that image. If you are with other people and feel too embarrassed to say it out loud, just say it silently to yourself. But, Do It!

Now for that yummy meal you've prepared. A balanced meal consists of:

**Protein** like chicken, beef, fish, tofu, eggs, or any other food high in protein.

**Vegetables**. The vegetables should be fresh. Rather than boiling your vegetables in water and losing many of the nutrients, try steaming them, lightly sautéing them, or roasting them. Add a half a yam or sweet potato for a powerful nutritious treat. You could start with a salad, or occasionally try finishing with that salad. The fiber from salad will push food through your system, and aid digestion.

# Whole Grains

Quinoa, or brown rice are an excellent choice with any green vegetable. Quinoa and brown rice also contain protein.

## Green Tea

Top off your meal with a hot cup of green tea. The substances in green tea increase levels of hormones that tell fat cells to break down fat. This releases fat into the bloodstream and makes it available as energy.

## After Dinner

Let your meal settle. This would be a perfect time to do some journaling. Did any challenges come up for you during the day? Write about it. If you

have kids or family to deal with, save your journaling for just before bedtime. Even if it's just a sentence or two, or a paragraph, try to write something. A lot of people write at different times. You might want to write in the mornings or on your breaks. Whatever you choose, Do It. You can also take this time to check off some of your boxes in your daily chart.

If this is your TV time, here are one or two more exercises you can do while you're watching your favorite show.

## Leg Lift Butt Tighteners

Get on your hands and knees with your legs hip distance apart. Keeping your knees bent and your foot flexed in a flat position, lift one leg at a time up behind you, foot towards the ceiling. Do this 25 times. Then switch legs. Repeat until you finish one hundred lifts.

## Side Variation

Hold your bended leg out to the side and while lifted, straighten it out ten times on each leg. Do three sets on each leg, or as many times as you can. It's important not to push yourself too hard especially if this is all new to you.

## Side Stretch

A side stretch can be done two different ways. One way is to put your right hand on your right hip, raise your left hand straight up as you reach to your right side as far as you can stretch. Repeat on the other side. Do this at least five times.

The other way is to stand two to three feet away from a wall. Repeat the stretch, only this time put your stretching hand flat against the wall and push for an extra stretch on your side.

## Bedtime

Now that you've done such a great job all day, add this one last thing before going to sleep. Close your eyes, and consciously release any challenges you might have had with events or people during the day. Bless them and release them, knowing that everything will work out for your highest good because you are aligned with a new energy that cooperates with you in every way.

## Do Your Gratitude Practice

Giving thanks for things in your life just before sleep has the added effect of letting it work more directly on your subconscious mind. Just before closing your eyes to sleep, tell yourself how grateful you are that you were able to take care of yourself today, and make positive changes in both mind and body. Be grateful that you are feeling healthier, stronger, and happier.

Repeat these affirmations:

*It gets easier for me to do healthy things for myself day after day.*

*I love my body, and I love how the changes I've made in body and mind are working for me.*

Then, if you haven't already done this, go to your checklist in the back of the book and check the boxes of the things you completed for the day.

## Now Go to Sleep

Sleep is the time your body gets to rest and regenerate. It's important to get at least seven or eight hours of sleep. The right amount of sleep at night energizes your body and brain, and helps you feel alert and focused during the day. Not getting enough sleep will cause your brain to release chemicals that signal hunger. This is why you might be feeling that you want to eat more and exercise less. Without the proper rest, both your body and your mind will be sluggish, and make your journey much more challenging. Get your rest.

## Chart

Below is your daily routine with boxes to check your progress. Don't be negative if you miss one or two things during your daily practice. Just remember the more boxes checked, the closer you are to that fabulous new you.

# THINGS I COMPLETED TODAY

- ☐ I did my morning gratitude session.
- ☐ I set the mood for my day.
- ☐ I incorporated all the exercises into my daily routine.
- ☐ I incorporated some of the exercises into my daily routine.
- ☐ I practiced my fire breath.
- ☐ I had no sugar today.
- ☐ I limited my sugar intake today.
- ☐ I followed the healthy food suggestions completely.
- ☐ I ate smaller portions than usual.
- ☐ I only ate healthy snacks.
- ☐ I repeated my affirmations at least five times or more.
- ☐ I did something to help improve my physical beauty.
- ☐ I followed my daily workout plan.
- ☐ I visualized and was able to see my desired body.
- ☐ I wrote in my journal.

---

**TIP**

At the end of the book I have lists, checklists, and products mentioned in the book for easy reference.

---

# CHAPTER 7:
# THE NINE-DAY LOSE FAT GAIN MUSCLE DIET

One day in the gym one of the trainers I knew walked up to me and asked me how I manage to keep my body toned. I told him about my Nine-Day Lose Fat Gain Muscle Diet. Nine days later he came back to me and said, "Hey, your diet really works! I feel leaner, lighter, and stronger in just nine days!" Needless to say, I was not surprised.

I have tried many things to get that finely toned look for my competitions. I would ask a lot of my competitors how they do it. I heard all kinds of methods for quick fat loss. After trying out most of them, I decided to create my own diet. I combined a number of methods and came up with the one that seems to work the best.

Usually, about four weeks before a competition I turn to my special diet. If you are not a competitor and just want to lose weight and put muscle on at the same time, or want to have a quick weight loss and still stay healthy, this will be the perfect diet for you too. This diet is high in protein and fiber and will burn the fat quickly.

## The Nine-Day Lose Fat Gain Muscle Diet Shopping List

- ☐ Wild caught salmon (you can get a frozen bag from Costco)
- ☐ Eggs (3 dozen)
- ☐ Asparagus
- ☐ Black beans (canned or dried)
- ☐ Sweet potatoes (4 to 6)
- ☐ Spinach
- ☐ String beans
- ☐ Sugar snap peas (fresh)
- ☐ Lentils
- ☐ Hummus (choose your flavors)
- ☐ Carrots
- ☐ Coconut oil

---

**TIP**
Always use a small plate.
Measure the portions to the size of the plate.

---

## THE DIET
## Days One, Two, and Three
## Breakfast

Scrambled eggs + Black beans

## Lunch
Salmon + Asparagus + Sweet potato

## Dinner
Lentil soup + Salmon + Carrots or Sweet potatoes + String beans or Broccoli

## Snacks
If you're hungry during the day or in the evening, have some lentil soup or snack on raw sweet peas, or a small handful of nuts or seeds.

## Days Four, Five, and Six Breakfast
Scrambled eggs (2 or 3) + Spinach

## Lunch
Chicken + Asparagus + Sweet potato

## Dinner
Lentil Soup + Chicken + Carrots + String beans or Broccoli

## Snacks
Lentil soup or snack on raw sweet peas, a small handful of nuts or seeds.

## Days Seven, Eight, And Nine Breakfast
Scrambled Eggs + Spinach

## Lunch
Shrimp or Mahi Mahi (or any whitefish) + ½ Yam or Sweet potato

## Dinner
Same fish choice as lunch + Carrots or Sweet potatoes + String beans or Broccoli

## Snacks
Lentil soup or snack on raw sweet peas, a small handful of nuts or seeds.

> **TIP**
> If you are getting results from this diet that excite you, and decide you want to do this diet for a longer period of time, I suggest you add salads after the first nine days for a few days. Then go back to the regular nine-day diet for nine more days.

## Affirmations for the Nine-Day Diet:

*Calories don't count when I am eating sensibly.*

*Knowing this is all healthy food, I know I am getting thinner with each meal I eat.*

*Eating this way becomes easier for me every day.*

REMEMBER: The best thing that you can do for yourself before eating any meal is to stop and affirm to yourself:

*Thank you for this healthy food. I know that it is helping me to create the healthy body I desire.*

This diet will burn fat and give you better tone for your muscles and adding these positive thoughts and images will make you stronger mentally. When you change your thinking, you WILL change your body.

# Chapter 8:
# Exercise

Wouldn't you want to be able to dance into your eighties, nineties, hundreds? My mother is one hundred and three now and she's still dancing, doing chair yoga, riding her bike, and going out to lunch every day. I'm sure one of the reasons is that she is happy living with us, and she's always stayed busy throughout her life. I've also kept her exercising her body and her mind for the past eight years. "Use it or lose it," as the saying goes. Just sitting all day is no longer an option. You've got to get your body moving.

Tests have proven that your brain also benefits from a good physical workout. Just two hours of aerobic exercise a week improves learning and verbal memory. That's only a minimum of twenty minutes a day for six days. And when you are doing affirmations and visualizations along with your exercises, you are getting a double whammy, and reach your goal faster.

Now it's time to start your daily workout plan. You can follow my daily routine for you in this book or choose one from my website. I have a full body workout that really sculpts your body, and another lighter workout for beginners and older enthusiasts that I did with my mother when she was one hundred years old. Yes, that's right. I said one hundred!

## Adapt Workouts to Meet Your Fitness Level

There are many ways to adapt the movements I use in my videos to fit a chair workout. The important thing is to do something to get your body moving towards your goal. If you are more experienced, then follow along with me on the video, and If you are a beginner or haven't exercised in a while, just follow along with my mom. You can do it. After all, if she could do this at one hundred, you can do it at your age. The workout I did with my mom has me on a mat and on the floor, but my mom was doing adaptations of the same workout with a chair.

There are also a lot of free workouts available on YouTube and all over the internet. Find one you like. If you have the money, join a gym. It's always a good idea to get out of the house and away from your everyday distractions so you can concentrate on your fitness. You can also use *Saba's Autosize* in your car to supplement your regular workouts.

---

**TIP**
**Start off slowly. Especially if you
haven't exercised in a while.**

---

I have had experience straining myself too much in an attempt to get back into shape in one day. It's just not possible. The Think It, Do It, Be It method is not an overnight program. It's a lifestyle. So, take it easy at first. I'm not the kind of personal trainer that will say, "Come on, move that butt! Push! Make it burn!" Remember I got my body into great shape just by eating right and doing a little something every day, while using affirmations and visualizations to help me believe I could reach my goal.

Remember to take the time to stretch and warm up your muscles. You will be less likely to experience muscle pain after a workout. You might feel a natural soreness, or I like to say a feeling that your muscles have been used, but they won't tighten up and cause you a lot of real pain later.

## Walking

Walking is fantastic exercise, and a great way to start if you are one of those people who has allowed your body to deteriorate, lose muscle tone, and gain a lot of extra weight. Walking not only is a natural way to exercise, but it acts as a massage for your inner organs and increases your energy level throughout the day. And the beautiful thing about it is that you don't need any special equipment. Sure, you can buy fancy walking shoes, but they aren't needed to get you out there and get you moving. Just start walking. Start by walking around the block. Enjoy seeing your neighborhood by foot.

Walking for twenty minutes to a half hour is enough to work your heart and feel good. But after you've gotten into the habit of walking, try increasing your walk to thirty or forty minutes. My adventurous husband used to hike up and down canyons in LA or find great parks to walk through to keep his walks interesting.

You can also use a treadmill at home or at a gym. Modern treadmills are amazing. You can program the exact kind of workout you want, and use them day or night, rain or shine.

Oh yeah, and while you're doing your workout don't talk on your cell phone. Do your affirmations instead. That will energize you and add more power to your workouts.

## Stationary Bikes

We have a stationary bike on our patio that we use when we can't get to the gym, or just want to ride while watching some TV. My one hundred and three-year old mother uses it two or three times a week when she doesn't go into use the bikes at the senior center. It's pretty much the same as walking. Twenty minutes is enough, but you can ride as long as you like.

## CLASSES

Gyms have all the equipment you'd ever need, and they have some great classes as well. Here are a few of my favorites:

## Yoga

Yoga is a great form of exercise that balances the body and the mind. You don't have to be super flexible to begin doing yoga. It's a practice that allows you to gain little by little while still getting benefits. Always do only what you are capable of and find alternative ways of doing difficult poses. You can always ask the instructors to help you.

Besides getting a great workout and adding to your flexibility, yoga is also known to be a healing form of exercise. It is known to lessen the pain from lower back injuries, arthritis, headaches, and all kinds of ailments.

Because the practice of yoga lowers the blood pressure and increases circulation, it lowers the risk of heart disease. Plus, learning how to breathe is always a good thing.

There are many kinds of yoga practiced in America. Too many to mention really, but generally they focus on putting the body into poses or stretches.

Personally, I prefer Kundalini yoga, which focuses more on spirituality and various types of breathing to go with the stretches. But look around, try one or two, and choose one you are drawn to.

## Mat Pilates

Pilates machines have been around for a long time and are built around resistance training using pulleys and springs. It's a terrific and extremely effective method of toning the entire body. The problem is that the machines are big and take up a lot of room. Gradually, some instructors started developing pilates classes you can do on a mat in a gym. I have been doing a mat pilates class twice a week for many years at the gym. I love it.

## Bodyworks Plus Abs

This is a class you can do using light weights or not. It is a tough class, but if you are young or in fairly good shape, this could be a great class for you. It not only sculpts and tones your body while you move to some highly-charged music that can really get you moving, it also gets your heart going. Just remember you don't have to listen to that young fit person in the front of the room yelling at you to, "Push it! Push it! Push it!" or "Come on, you can do it!" Know yourself. Maybe you can't. Especially if you are just starting out or older. To start, you could work out at least three times a week. You can always step it up a bit when you feel comfortable enough to do so.

## Zumba

Zumba is a great form of aerobic exercise, especially if you are into the Latin beat. If you like to dance, you'll love this way of working your body out. It's like going to a party and having fun. It's really good for your heart and moves every part of your body at the same time. You don't have to be great at it, just try and follow along with the instructor and do the best you can. You will be getting benefit out of any kind of movement you can do.

## Water Aerobics

This is one of my favorites, especially in the summer when you can take a class outside. This is a full body cardio and muscle workout. Because you are in the water, you are using a water resistance method of strengthening your body. It makes everything you do easier, which is why it is recommended for a lot of seniors. It can be as hard or as easy of a workout as you want. The benefits of a water aerobics class are that you are burning calories and reducing blood pressure while you are working every muscle in your body with ease.

Gyms also have other classes you could try like, **Cross-Fit**, **Boxing**, and **Step Aerobics** classes, or **Spinning,** which is stationary bike riding in a group, and usually pretty strenuous and a real calorie burner. Find one that you like, and fit it into your schedule

Working out and moving your body is a big part of Do It.

# Dealing with Exercise Pain

After a strenuous workout, your muscles might be tight in various parts of your body. For me, it's usually in my shoulders and upper back. I know sometimes, especially when I'm getting ready for a competition, I push a little harder than usual. Sometimes the stress on my muscles can also give me a headache. It's difficult reaching your neck and shoulders to massage those painful areas. But fear not, there is a tool that is perfect for getting at those hard to reach areas. It is an S shaped metal thing with little wooden balls on each end. It's called a Thera Cane, and it costs about $39.99 or less at Relax the Back stores. You can also find it at Brookstone, online, or at many massage and sporting goods stores. It has eased my pain and healed many sore muscles for me.

If you can't afford a Thera Cane, buy a tennis ball for about $1.00, place it on the floor in your home, lie down and move your body over the ball to press in on your painful areas. There are also shiatzu massage machines available at many stores, or massage wands that are relatively inexpensive. We have a really great one called the Pure Wave handheld massager. It's a little more expensive than most wands, but it's extremely effective, and has changeable speeds and massage heads. It's available online. Just Google "Pure Wave Massager."

Foam rollers are the new rage. They were created by Cassidy Phillips, an athlete, who in his prime, was diagnosed with fibromyalgia. Not believing he could be held back, he started playing around with things that would ease his pain. He created these foam rollers to massage and stimulate his trigger points and speed up muscle recovery. This process is also called myofascial release. It helps break down the fascia tissue that surrounds the muscle and allows the muscle to relax.

The foam roller is out there starting at $9.99. If you are on a budget you can do what I did. I picked up a rolling pin from the 99 Cents store, and wrapped it in packing foam that I got from a foam store for 25 cents. It worked pretty well. Just be sure to wash it before you bake your next batch of cookies. Ha ha.

## Saunas, Jacuzzis, and Massage

A really inexpensive way to relax those tired muscles is to sit in the sauna for twenty minutes after your workout. If you don't belong to a gym, just relax in a hot bath with one cup of Epsom salts. And of course, if you can afford it, a good massage will always help to relax sore muscles.

# CHAPTER 9:
## SABA'S AUTOSIZE

My hope is that you can make *Autosize* another prac-tice to help you reach your goal.

## How to Do *Autosize*

With each picture below is an affirmation, visualization, and explanation. Repeating the affirmation with each exercise will speed up the process by helping your mind reinforce what is going on with your body. Doing it whenever your car is in a stopped position is important. Soon *Autosize* will become second nature to you, and keep you off your cell phone, which has been proven to be a danger in your car. So, instead of something dangerous, why not do something healthy in your car?

> **TIP**
> Remember, *Autosize* only during down time while waiting in your car. NEVER while the car is moving or in traffic NEVER WHILE THE CAR IS MOVING OR I TRAFFIC TRAFFIC.

In some of the illustrations I use something I call an auto wheel. It is also called a pilates ring. I use it so you can get a clear picture of how to place your hands on your steering wheel. If you like, you can buy a ring like the one in the illustrations. I carry mine in the car along with a few elastic stretch cords, so when I am a passenger I can still get in a workout in the car. I find this comes in handy when I'm on a long car ride with someone. They are doing the driving and I'm getting in a workout. Sweet.

## Stretching

Stretching is a very important part of working out. You can use these stretches before or after you *Autosize.*

## Visualization

## Visualize your muscles relaxing and lengthening.

## Affirmation:

*I let my body relax as I let go of stress and tension.*

## Body Stretch Outside Your Car

This is a great stretch for your lower back and hamstrings. Before you even get into your car, open your car door and place your foot on the bottom door runner. Place your other foot behind you with your toes pointing forward. Keeping both legs straight (but not locked), bend over to reach for the ankle of the leg on the car. Let yourself fall into the stretch as far as you can without forcing it. Count to 10, and reverse legs to stretch the other leg.

If you are really limber, place your foot on the hood of your car and then reach for your toes.

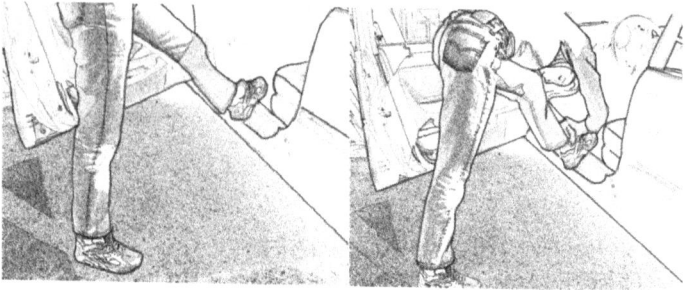

# Head and Neck Stretch

Sit up straight and relax your hands on your lap. Stretch your head down trying to touch your chin to your chest. This will be your center position. Now slowly roll your head up to look as far as you can over your right shoulder. Slowly go back to the center position and roll your head up to look over your left shoulder. Don't push yourself, just go as far as you can with ease. Repeat 3 times.

Remember to be very gentle with your neck.

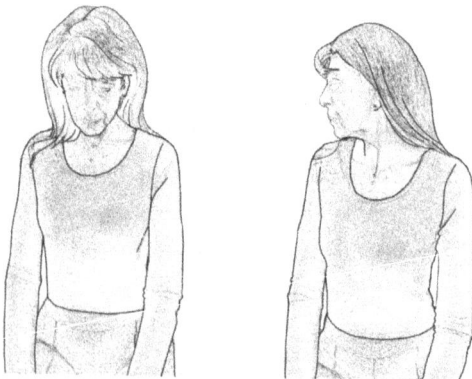

## Shoulder Shrugs

Sit up straight. Relax your arms to your sides and lift your shoulders up as if you were trying to touch your ears. Hold for a second, then allow your shoulders to drop down. Repeat 3 to 5 times.

## Shoulders Rolls

Sit up straight. In the same position as your shoulder shrugs, with your arms relaxed at your side, roll your shoulders forward in a circular motion. Do this 3 to 5 times, and then reverse and roll your shoulders backwards 3 to 5 times.

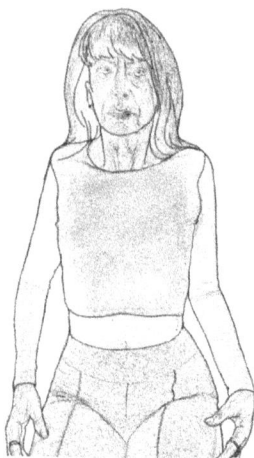

# Back Stretch 1

Sit up straight and place your hands flat on the roof of your car. Walk your hands back towards the rear of your car as far as you can. Feel the stretch in your arms, shoulders, and upper back. Just stretch as far as you can without straining your arms or back. Hold for 5 seconds.

## Back Stretch 2

This is sometimes called the Cat-Cow stretch. Sit up straight and grab your steering wheel at 9 and 3. Push your chest towards the steering wheel and stretch your neck and head back like a swaybacked cow. Then reverse the stretch by caving in your chest and abdomen while lowering your neck and head like a stretching cat. Do this at least 5 times for a good relaxing stretch for your upper body.

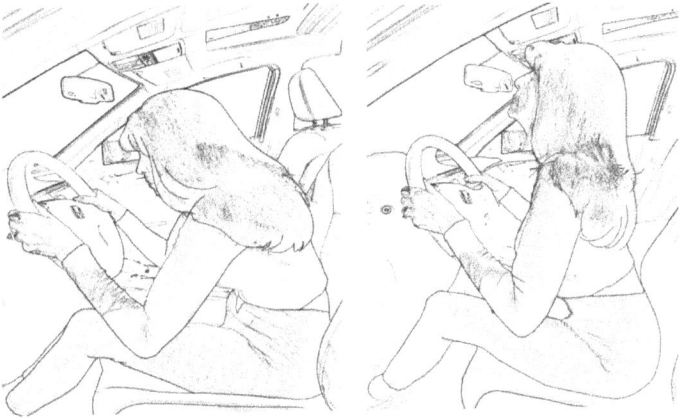

## Trunk Twist

Put your hands in prayer position. Now drop your left hand to your side, and keeping your right arm bent in prayer position, twist your trunk to the left as far as possible. Just go as far as you can without strain. Then go back to prayer position, drop your right arm and twist to the left. Hold the stretch for 10 seconds.

## Side Stretch

Sit up straight. Reach your right arm and hand over your head and bend at the waist trying to touch your driver's side window. Feel the stretch on your right side. Hold for 5 to 10 seconds. Then reverse the stretch bending at the waist and reaching your left hand and arm over your head as far as you can to the right for 5 to 10 seconds.

After you've stretched out, you are ready for the exercises.

## THE EXERCISES

Every *Autosize* exercise is done either as pulses or as a hold to the count of 10. If it helps, put on some motivating music. Remember, every minute counts.

## Chest

Here are three *Autosize* exercises for your chest.

## Visualization

**Visualize the chest you would like to have. See a well-shaped chest lifting and getting firmer and stronger with every pulse or hold.**

## Affirmation:

*As I strengthen my chest, I strengthen my resolve.*

## Chest Exercise 1

Using your wheel like a clock, place your wrists at nine and three, as pictured in the illustration, and squeeze your wrists against the steering wheel. Hold or pulse.

## Chest Alternative

From the same position, grab the wheel with your hands at nine and three, pick your elbows up, round your back, and try to push your hands towards each other.

## Chest Exercise 2

Without using your steering wheel, lift your arms up parallel to the ground in a prayer position. Now, place your right fist into the palm of your left hand, and wrap your left hand around your right as in the illustration. Push your hands against each other for 10 counts, then switch hands and repeat. Repeat your visualization and affirmation.

## Chest Exercise 3

Here's another one you can use without your steering wheel.

Put your hands in a prayer position with your elbows lifted. Pushing the heels of your palms together, slowly raise your arms above your head while keeping a steady pressure. Then slowly lower your arms until they are in front of your chest again. Repeat your visualization and affirmation.

## Arms

I have created a number of *Autosize* arm exercises. Choose the ones you like, or be like me and use them all.

## Visualization

**Visualize a sleek, tight, shapely arm. The way it used to be or the way you desire it to be.**

## Affirmation:
*My arms are tight and shapely.*

## Arms Exercise 1: Inner Arms and Pecs

Bend your arms and lean forward to place your forearms along the outside of the steering wheel. Straighten
your back and push your arms toward each other. This
will put emphasis on your inner arms.

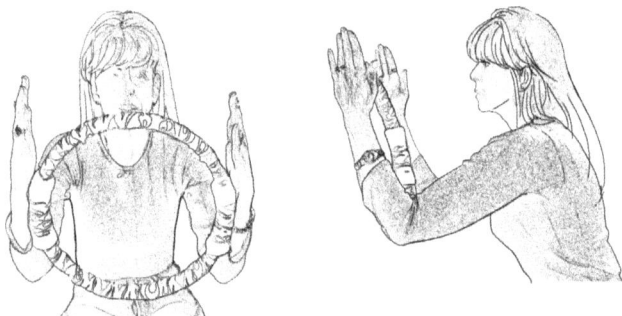

---

**TIP**
If you want to work your arms, be sure
your back is straight. If you want to work
your chest, round your back into a C shape,
and do the same *Autosize* exercise.

---

## Arms Exercise 2: Outer Arms plus Legs

Place your wrists on the inside of the wheel at nine
and three, palms facing away from each other and
push out.

If you can't use your steering wheel to do this:

With your knees about a foot apart, straighten your arms and slide them between your knees with your palms facing away from each other.

Straighten your back, and try to push your knees together while resisting with your arms.

# Arms Exercise 3: Outer Arms plus Legs

Do the same thing as #3 only turn your palms to face each other as you push your legs out.

## Abs

Your abs, or abdominal muscles, support your back, and the stronger your abs, the tighter your central core.

## Visualization

**Visualize yourself with a tight, flat stomach.**

## Affirmation:

*I feel my power as I strengthen my core.*

## Abs Exercise

Place your palms on the top of your knees, keeping your arms either bent or straight. Round your back into a C shape and raise your toes up as you push down on your knees focusing on tightening your stomach.

## Thighs and Glutes

Who doesn't want a well-rounded gluteus maximus? Or as some people call it, your butt. This *Autosize* exercise helps tighten your butt and the back of your thighs at the same time.

## Visualization

**Visualize your thighs getting tighter and firmer and your glutes getting rounder and tighter.**

## Affirmation:

*I am developing magnificent glutes and thighs.*

## Thighs and Glutes Exercise

Push your seat back and lower the back of your seat as far as you can. Lie back keeping your arms on the side of your seat or hold them up to increase the intensity of the exercise. Lift your hips up by pushing your heels firmly into the floor. With each lift tighten your buttocks. Don't worry if you can't lift too high at first. It's still working.

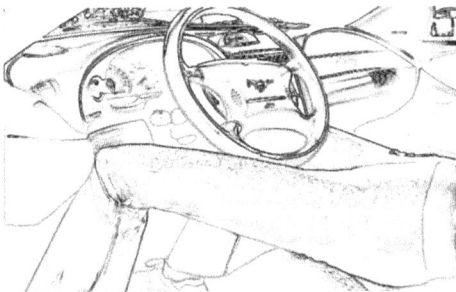

# Legs

Strong legs give you a strong foundation and propel you forward.

## Visualization

**Visualize stronger, shapelier legs.**

## Affirmation:

*As I shape and strengthen my legs, I move forward with ease.*

## Inner Thighs

Have your legs two or three feet apart. Put your arms in prayer position and put your elbows on the inside of your knees keeping your arms pointing forward. Now try to close your legs as you resist with your arms.

## Outer Thighs

For your outer thigh do the exact same thing, only place your elbows on the outside of your knees and try to open your legs as you resist.

## Upper Thigh and Calf

Push your seat back as far as possible. Working one leg at a time, place your hands on your thigh just above your knee. Flex your foot towards you to increase tension on your calf muscle, as you straighten your leg while lifting it as far as possible. You can feel the thigh and hips working. Now switch legs.

---

**TIP**

**Be sure to keep your back straight to get the full benefit for your legs. If your back is in a C shape, you will only be working your arms and chest.**

---

## Neck

The firmer your neck, the more youthful you look.

## Visualization
**Visualize a smooth and elegant neck.**

## Affirmation:
*My head sits atop a strong and elegant neck.*

## Neck Exercise

Sit up straight, bend your head back as far as it can go, and point your face towards the roof of your car. Open your mouth and tighten your jaw as you slowly close your mouth. Do this at least 25 times until you can work up to 100. This one is not only working on firming your neck, it's also helping to get rid of that double chin you might have developed.

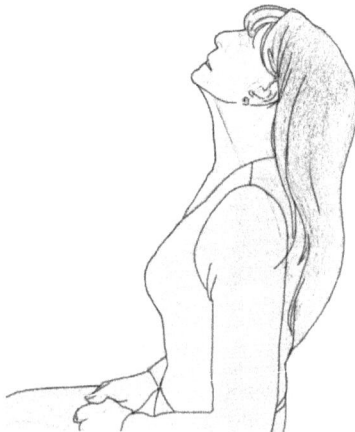

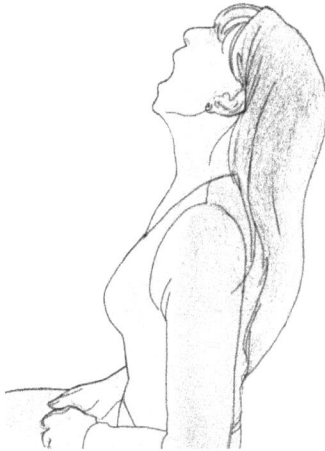

## Fingers, Wrists, and Hands

Most people forget to exercise their fingers, hands, and wrists. They are a big part of keeping strong and youthful along with the rest of the body.

Also, exercising your wrists and hands will help prevent carpel tunnel injuries. I use a foam stress ball to press my fingers against, but I have given you an alternative if you can't find a foam stress ball.

## Visualization
**Visualize your fingers and hands looking smooth and youthful.**

## Affirmation:
*My hands and wrists are smooth and flexible.*
    **And...**
*I can now open jars easier!*

# Fingers

Keeping your fingers as straight as you can, press each finger against the ball or just your thumb if you don't have a ball, and hold for the count of 2. You can do both hands at the same time or just concentrate on one at a time. Your choice.

# Wrists and Hands 1

Put your hands in a claw-like position as if you were a cat trying to scratch something. You can either hold your arms out straight or keep them bent. It's a slightly different stretch in either position. Now, in the claw position, bend your hands backwards at the wrist as far as you can get them. Then, still in claw position, bend them down as far down as you can go. To start, you can do this in 3 sets of 5 counts.

## Wrists and Hands 2

Put your hands in the claw position, and circle them in
outside circles going away from each other. Do this for 5

turns and reverse your hands the opposite way circling towards the inside. Repeat this 3 to 5 times and work up to 10 times on each hand.

If you are doing this for the first time, you will probably hear a lot of crackly noises going on. Don't let it scare you. Once your wrists and hands get used to this, the sounds will go away.

That's it. You just learned how to do a complete workout with *Saba's Autosize*. Once you learn these *Autosize* exercises, you can do any section, anywhere, anytime as you sit in your own personal mobile gym. Do your visualizations and affirmations and repeat them as you *Autosize*. Remember, when it comes to getting in shape, every minute counts.

# Chapter 10:
# Youthful Body and Skin

Being a champion Bikini Diva, I've learned that keeping your entire body youthful is both an inside and an outside job. It's a job because if you want to look youthful for life, it's going to take some concentrated effort and dedication. I've heard it said that, "From birth to fifty your body is a gift from God, and from fifty on up your body is a gift to yourself." I know most of you have no desire to be a Bikini Diva, but I'm betting you still want to look good, with the best body you can have, while living the healthiest life possible. That's why I included this section in the book.

There's nothing like being a senior and having a body with a smooth, youthful glow to it. You will look years younger if you have healthy smooth skin.

Sometimes I'll be walking along the beach, and a young guy will come up from behind me to start a conversation. When he reaches me, he'll say something like, "Hi! Oh, sorry I thought you were someone else." I laugh as I learn that the reason they stopped me was because they were attracted to my youthful looking body. And then when I turned around, they could see that I wasn't a young woman. A lot of the guys go on talking to me anyway, thinking I'm in my forties or fifties. I'll admit it is kind of an ego boost to see their shocked reaction when they find out how old I really am. They usually follow up by asking how I stay in such good shape.

Both in and out of the gym, younger women want me to share any secrets I have on how to keep a youthful looking body. I love seeing their enthusiasm when I remind them that if I can keep my body youthful without any surgical procedures at this age, anyone can. Here are a few things I have used to keep this seventy-five year old body looking much more youthful.

By using the Think It, Do It, Be It method, and filling your body with clean healthy foods, you might grow older, but you won't get old. You will naturally find your body developing a more youthful glow. But if you really want to turn back the clock on aging, you will want to look at all of the interesting things on the following pages. This section of the book is reserved for learning about how you can make some choices to beautify the outside of your body.

## Making Your Own Products for Less

If you want to do nice things for yourself but feel like all those products you need are too expensive, you're right. The pampering most men and women do for themselves is very costly. If you are one of those who can afford it, that's wonderful. Go for it. But for those of you who are not as comfortable spending, there are simple and less costly ways of creating what you need. As I progressed on my journey, I went through periods of having money and not having money. So one of the things that I tried to do was to figure out how to make expensive things affordable. After I experienced using these products, I created some inexpensive products of my own that achieved the same results. After all, everyone has the right to feel beautiful no matter the size of your bank account. Let's start by looking at the body from top to bottom starting with your skin.

## Your Skin

Eating the right foods is always the first and most important step in keeping your body looking and functioning as youthfully as possible. But don't stop there. Exercise tones the muscles beneath the outer layer of skin and helps to plump the skin so that it doesn't look so wrinkly and saggy. But you need to help the outer body by giving the skin the right nutrients to stay as elastic as possible. You must always take care of your skin by treating it to healthy high-quality creams and lotions that hydrate and soften. You deserve to treat yourself well.

## Saba's Body Scrub

This is something you can do for yourself in the comfort of your own home. The ingredients for this mixture will cost you around a dollar a month, and will usually last longer than a year if kept refrigerated.

You'll need:

One cup of coffee grounds One cup of sugar

One cup of sea salt

One cup of coconut oil or extra virgin olive oil

Mix the coffee, sugar, and salt together until blended. Then add your softened coconut oil or extra virgin olive oil and mix it in well until it is all blended together.

This recipe is also available on my website in the Tips Section under "Cellulite Basher."

## How to Use It

You can either go outside or stand in a shower to apply this mixture to your body because it is a little messy and slippery. So be sure to have good footing when applying it. If you are doing this for a beauty treatment, then apply it all over your body, and rub it in for a few minutes before you wash it off with warm water.

If you are using it to get rid of unwanted cellulite, place the mixture on your body where you have cellulite, and rub it into the area, in either a circular or up and down motion, for fifty to one hundred strokes. Then wash it off with warm water. If you are using it as a scrub for youthful looking skin, you can use this mixture as many times a week as you like.

This scrub mixture will save you a lot of money and last for months. I put a small amount in a container and take it to the gym with me. I keep the rest in a tightly sealed container in the fridge.

## Use It in the Sauna

Scrub your body down with the mixture, and then sit in the sauna for about twenty minutes. I prefer sitting in the sauna to let the heat open my pores so my body can more fully absorb the nutrients and oils. Then lie back and enjoy your treatment. You can rinse off in the shower and walk around the rest of the day feeling softer and more beautiful.

Warning: Make sure there are non-skid surfaces in the sauna. You don't want anyone slipping on the oils.

The same benefits might be had by using it outside on a warm sunny day and relaxing for a few minutes after applying it.

You can also wrap the sections you really want to concentrate on in plastic cling wrap and leave it on for a half hour to an hour. This allows it to really soak into your body and smooth your skin like you've had a day at the spa.

If you don't have the time, you can just scrub it on and rinse it off. Your skin will still get a wonderful benefit from the treatment.

## The Wrap

The body wrap from It Works! is a body-contouring product that works when you wrap it around various parts of your body. It's for tightening the skin on the neck, stomach, arms, face, or any part of your body you want to be firmer. It contains all-natural ingredients, reduces cellulite, and tightens and firms your skin, taking you from flab to fab.

I started using the body wrap on my problem area in 2014. Everyone has a problem area, an area of your body that you consider woefully deficient, flabby, wrinkled, riddled with cellulite, or just plain ugly. Most of the time no one else notices or cares about this problem area except you. But since it's your body, you're the only one that matters.

My problem area is my upper arms. Some people call it the wave muscle, or the "flap-wings." When my grandson

Ryan was little, he used to love to hit those flaps, and laugh as they jiggled. I lifted weights to firm up the muscles underneath, and it helped a lot, but it took over a year, and there was still a little bit of residual loose skin and fat that wouldn't go away. I put extra-added attention on my upper arms and did all kinds of exercise that specialized in firming up that particular muscle. Then I discovered the wrap. I noticed a difference right away. I didn't have to use it long before my flap-wings got tighter and more toned. They are still my challenge area, but the wrap combined with pushups and arm exercises keep it in check.

My best friend had a belly fat challenge. She used the wrap and her belly got tighter and flatter. I recently started using it on my neck. It's an outstanding product that can be used on any problem area on your body. Another advantage to the wrap is that you can have it on under your clothes as you go about your daily routine.

A treatment can last twenty minutes, or however long you want. Sometimes I sleep in it, depending on if my husband falls asleep first, or on how frisky he feels. Once right before I had a red carpet event, my upper arms looked a little crepey to me. I wrapped my arms for a couple of hours and my arms were as smooth as could be for the event. If you fall in love with this product like I have, you can easily become a distributor and earn some money introducing it to others. http://sabasfitforlife.myitworks.com/

# Red Light Therapy

The first thing I asked when someone mentioned this to me was, "What the heck is red light therapy, and what does it do?" By doing research and using red light therapy, here's what I found out. Plants absorb their light from the sun. Red light therapy removes the harmful UV (ultra violet) light rays which allows our body to soak up the beneficial rays that help to reduce fine lines, wrinkles, sun damage, and skin problems like acne and psoriasis. The process is like lying in a tanning bed, only the lights in the bed are red lights. Just a twelve-minute session three times a week can regenerate old cells. Red light therapy has been known to stimulate and energize the body's natural process.

If you are new to red light treatments and have the time, it's a good thing to go daily for two weeks when you start. I try to go about five times a week, but three or four times a week for twelve minutes at a time would be fine too.

The cost for this depends on where you live. I pay $55 a month for unlimited use. It used to be more expensive, but as it became more popular the price has gone down. Most places charge more, but you can still find multi-use packages for less if you Google it. When my husband and I went to Wisconsin to visit his family, their local gym had red light therapy for free as part of the membership. So check around for the best prices.

If you live in Los Angeles, or if you are vacationing here, you can visit the Sun Spa. They have salons in Sherman Oaks, Glendale, and Northridge. If you're ever in LA, stop by the Sherman Oaks Sun Spa for a visit. The owners know me, and If you mention my name, they will give you one free red light therapy treatment along with any treatment you buy. Now that's a sweet deal.

I also have a handheld red light therapy wand. You can find them available on the internet, and the cost ranges from \$60 to \$400. After a lot of research, I've found that the \$60 one does the same job as the more expensive ones. I use this when I travel. It's a great tool to take with you on vacations, or to use when you can't get to the red light therapy beds. If you can't afford the treatments and still feel you want to get the benefit of red light therapy, the wand does the same job but it covers only a few inches at a time.

---

**TIP**
**ALWAYS protect your eyes when**
**doing red light therapy.**

---

# Infrared Light Therapy

Infrared light is another form of light energy, but infrared has more healing properties, goes deeper into the body, and will help you lose weight and detoxify and heal more quickly. Infrared therapy breaks up toxins and fats that are trapped in your body and forces your body to sweat it out. It also causes an increased blood flow which can heal injuries and is a great choice if you suffer from diabetes.

# More Therapies to Fit Your Budget

If your budget doesn't allow you the luxury of the handheld wand or red light therapy sessions, don't feel neglected. Here are some alternative and relatively inexpensive ways to treat your body to the conditioning and pampering it deserves.

# Massage

Massage is also a wonderful thing you can do for your entire body. You can go to a school that teaches massage for only $12 to $20 or get a light upper body massage in many malls for $1 a minute. There are day spas that range from $20 to $100 a day, or membership massage stores like Massage Envy that offer discounts for monthly members. You can also find great deals for massage and all kinds of other beauty treatments on Groupon.

# Baths

If you live in a small town or don't have access to massage schools, malls, or massage parlors, you can get a similar effect of a relaxing massage by taking a bath in Epsom salts. It's a great way to relax, and it's a wonderful skin softener too. You can spend as much as you like on more expensive bath soaks, but regular Epsom salts cost under $10 for a three-pound bag. And it lasts a very long time.

There are so many healthy choices available for pampering your skin and body from the most expensive to the least expensive. What's important is that you start treating your body like the temple it is. Start right away by doing something nice for your body. You'll feel and look better and more youthful, and when you feel better, you'll want to keep it that way.

# Hair and Scalp

Let's face it, if your hair is bright and bouncy it gives you a younger appearance. One day a few years ago, I looked in the mirror, and pulled my hair out of my ponytail. To my dismay, it didn't flop down gracefully

onto my shoulders like on the TV ads. It just stuck straight out. It was tired of being dyed, dried, and dry curled. I decided my hair needed some special care. I wanted to see if I could bring back the luster and youthful look it used to have. After all, if at this age I could do that with my body, why not my hair?

Most women reach a certain age and decide to cut their hair off because it's easier to care for. Not me. I enjoy having long hair. Probably because I could never grow my hair when I was younger. It would get to a certain length, and then just stop right below my shoulders. All my girlfriends had beautiful, flowing long hair. Why couldn't I?

Since I changed my diet and started caring for my hair in a different way, lo and behold, as a senior I finally reached the point where my hair is shiny, vibrant, and even grows faster.

I started by brushing my hair. I counted one hundred strokes; twenty-five for each quadrant of my head. I repeated my affirmations:

**What I am doing for my hair is bringing back the youthful look.**

I also affirmed:

**My hair and scalp are getting healthier with every stroke.**

I envisioned what my hair would look like when I got it in shape. I kept the affirmations and the visualizations in my consciousness and brushed my hair as much as I could during the day. If I had trouble getting to it during the day, I would always force myself to do it at night.

---

**TIP**
**Trim your hair often for healthier hair.**

---

I also switched shampoos to Ovation. I have found Ovation to be one of the best over-the-counter products for my hair. I used Ovation shampoo, conditioner, and the cell therapy product as well. The package of all three is $54.95, but it was well worth it. If your hair is in really bad shape and looks dry and listless right now, I suggest you use Ovation to initially get your hair back into the youthful shape you knew in your twenties.

Once your hair is in good condition, I have found that you only need to shampoo with Ovation once a month. When you do your weekly shampoo, it is good to use a different brand. A single bottle of Ovation can last about a year if you use it sparingly. So, it turned out to be a very good investment. After just a few short months, the shine was back, and when I took out the hair tie from my ponytail, my hair bounced down over my shoulders just like the TV ads. The feeling I got from seeing that totally justified the cost of using a really good shampoo and conditioner.

Now I switch off between Garnier and one of the inexpensive shampoos from the list below. I used Ovation once a month for the first year, but I don't use it at all any more. The cost of Garnier shampoo and conditioner is around $3.99. And it works just great at maintaining my healthy and shiny hair. Oh, and here's a little tip I picked up from hair specialists:

---

**TIP**
**Experts say it is healthier for**
**your hair to switch shampoo and**
**conditioner every six months.**

---

If you're looking for an organic shampoo, Natures Paradise is a great choice. It's a bit pricey starting at around $15, but you can look around in most health food stores and find natural shampoos starting at $3.50.

## Best Inexpensive Shampoos and Conditioners

If your hair is dry or brittle, try Pantene Pro-V Nature Fusion Smooth Vitality Shampoo for only $4.

For curly or wavy hair, there's Garnier Fructis at $5.

Herbal Essence is great for making fine hair look thicker at $5. And if you have treated hair, Vive Pro by L'Oreal will perk up your highlights for $13.

You can also find some great deals for shampoo at the Dollar Store. But wherever you decide to shop for your shampoo, please be sure to read the labels and make sure you are not buying shampoo that can harm your hair. Here's is a list of things you don't want in the shampoo you are buying:

- Phthalates
- Sulfates
- Parabens
- Triethanolamine

If you use conditioner, the best ones are Pantene, for regular hair. But if you have a challenge with frizz or have treated hair, you might choose Frizz Ease, Tresemme, Infusium, or Herbal Essence. These all range from $4 to $6.00.

---

**TIP**
**When your hair is wet use a comb,**
**not a brush. A brush will pull your**
**hair out, and you don't want that.**

---

## Hair treatments

Another way to bring back some of the lost luster or to take care of your split ends or frizz, is to treat your hair to a deep oil treatment. Going to a salon can cost anywhere from $85 to $190. If you are having a cost challenge, try using coconut oil and mayonnaise. It works just as well, and costs only pennies a day.

# Who Shouldn't Use Coconut Oil as a Hair Treatment

Here are some things you should know about how to use coconut oil on your hair, and if you should be using it at all.

Although this did not happen to me, if you have coarse, dry hair using coconut oil might not be a good idea for you. If you have that type of hair, you probably already have enough protein in it. Adding more with coconut oil could make your hair more brittle and cause it to break. It would be better for you to use olive oil, marula, or argan oil on your hair. For me those are the best, but you can also check out jojoba, rosemary essential, avocado, or pomegranate seed oils.

# How to Apply Oil to Hair

If you go to the gym, put the treatment on your hair, cover it with a shower cap, and sit in the sauna. Because of heat in the sauna, ten minutes should do it. You only need to do this once a month to keep your hair shiny and youthful. It's okay to do it twice a month if you have very damaged hair, but no more. Your hair doesn't really need it any more than that.

---

**TIP**
**Apply oil to damp hair.**

---

At home, you can apply the oil and put a shower cap over your hair and/or wrap it in a towel. Heat helps the hair absorb the oils, so this is a great thing to do in the summer while you are sitting outside catching up on some reading, gardening, or just soaking in the sun.

Argan and marula oil will cost you anywhere from $14 – $50. But extra virgin olive oil starts at around $3 and could go up to $15 depending on where you shop.

## Losing Hair?

It happens sometimes. Here's a little trick my mom did, when she turned one hundred and one. She felt she was losing too much of her beautiful white curly hair. While she was sitting around watching TV or in the car, she would just take her hair a section at a time and pull on it. Believe it or not, even at a hundred and one years of age, this worked. By stimulating her hair and scalp, she brought the thickness back, and eliminated those balding spots. I guess the old saying; "use it or lose it" really applies here. Plus, it was free!

## The Face

Just like your body, when your face loses muscle tone it starts to sag, wrinkles appear, and your skin begins to look tired. There are many ways to help slow down the aging process on your face. Here are a few of them. Use them along with this affirmation:

*My face radiates the health and beauty within.*

## Soft and Youthful Face

Everyone has their favorite creams, ointments, scrubs, masks, and moisturizers. I think most of the inexpensive ones work just as well as the ones that cost you a fortune. Plus there are some natural things you can use on both your body and your face that are affordable. Sometimes I wash my face with Murad Essential C. It costs me $36, but you don't have to use much, and mine will last me a full year, and sometimes longer.

I remember a high school girlfriend of mine who had such a beautifully clear face with skin like peaches and cream. Her sisters and mother were the same. One day I asked her mother what her secret was. I never forgot her answer. "I never wash my face," she said. "What?" I couldn't believe what I had just heard. She went on, "If you want to have a soft beautiful face, never wash it with soap." Then she explained that both she and her daughters would rinse their faces with water, but when it came to removing makeup or cleansing the face, they only used creams. Ever since that day I never put soap to my face again, and my complexion has always been flawless, except of course for that occasional zit that always seemed to pop up when my wonderful moon cycle was about to start.

When that happened, I would use a simple scrub right on the spot around three or four times during the day, and by the evening it would be gone.

At seventy-five, thankfully, I haven't had to worry about that in years.

When I wash my face, I use a facial cleanser that does not contain soap or ingredients in soap, like sodium lauryl sulfate, fragrances, colors, parabens, or DEAs. I wash twice a day, in the morning and at night. I use an inexpensive face wash that I get on sale at Marshall's.

Using a moisturizer is one of the kindest things you can do for your face. Moisturizing keeps your face from getting dry and wrinkly. It helps to keep that youthful supple look. Have you ever seen an apple that is left out to dry? Need I say more? I not only use a moisturizer under my makeup, but on days when I don't wear makeup, I apply moisturizer to my face at least three or four times a day.

I've used so many moisturizers during the years, but the ones that seem to work best for the skin on my face are Murad and Eucerin Daily Protection moisturizer. Radiance Cream from Touch and Glow works just as well, and costs under $10 verses $65 for Murad. So depending on the size of your wallet, there it is.

If this sounds like it's too expensive, you can always take a trip to Marshall's or some other discount department store and look through their facial products. You can pick up things there that usually cost from $60 to a few hundred dollars, for under $10. I've been known to pick up product there for $4 that even online, would cost $50.

## Keeping Your Face Youthful

There are many face creams on the market that promise to reduce your wrinkles, smooth your skin, and give you a more youthful-looking face. Some of these products do work in helping to slow down the aging process. If you have it, you can spend tons of money on all these creams and products. But if you don't have the money, you can get the same results inexpensively and naturally. Here are some easy and natural things I have used for my face that brought immediate, noticeable changes.

## Face Scrubs

There are so many ways to scrub your face. But a great idea is to keep it natural. By the way, it's also the cheaper way. For instance, honey and sugar in equal parts is a wonderful way to scrub your face. After you scrub it in, just leave it on for a few minutes before rinsing for a great natural, youthful look.

## Face Masks

Weekly face masks are very healthy for your skin. After a pack is on your face you can relax, watch a movie, or write a book. I say that because I'm wearing a face mask right now.

I use a generic cucumber peel because I like the feeling of pulling the peel off my face. Every once in a while, I will use just plain cucumbers on my face. But If you choose to go natural, just put a mixture of some honey and cucumber together and you have a completely natural mask that does the same thing. And as we've seen in many movies, just put a couple of slices of cucumbers or wet tea bags on your puffy eyes and the swelling will disappear.

Here is a list of things that you probably already have in your home and can use to make a fabulous face pack. Plus, they are the perfect solution, especially if you are on a tight budget.

## Raw Organic Honey

Honey is perfect for slowing down or stopping the wrinkles on your face because of its antioxidants. Combine one tablespoon of honey and four tablespoons of water. Stir them until they are blended well. Put it on your face, relax, and let it dry. Rinse it off with warm water.

---

**TIP**
**Double up on the measurements so you'll have enough for your neck.**

---

**TIP**
**Remember not to sit outside around bees. Ha ha.**

---

## Banana

If you are looking for an incredible way to keep those wrinkles away, you can combine your 1 tablespoon of raw honey with a ½ teaspoon of lemon juice, and combine those two ingredients with one ripe banana. The combination of the vitamin C, E, and potassium will do the trick for sure.

---

**TIP**
**Make sure your banana is ripe.**

---

## Papaya

When I was in India I learned one of the secrets to keeping those beautiful Indian complexions. A woman I met told me her secret and now I will share it with you.

Puree a soft small ripe papaya and add 2 tablespoons of honey and a teaspoon of lemon juice. Make sure it is mixed well, and then simply put it on your face as you would a regular mask. Leave it on until it is dry. Rinse it off with warm water, and for a wonderful feeling do another rinse with cold water.

## Avocados

Don't just throw the avocado peel away after you've treated yourself to this delicious fruit. Just take the residue of the fruit left on the peel to lightly rub it all over your face and neck. Leave it on for fifteen minutes, rinse it off with warm water, and voila, your face has been nourished with natural goodness.

There are so many natural fruits and vegetables that you can use to help keep your face looking more youthful. These are just the ones that I have tried.

---

**TIP**
**Be sure to find out what works best for oily or dry skin.**

---

**TIP**
**Don't forget your neck. Whatever you are doing for your face, do for your neck.**

---

## FACE CHALLENGES AND MASKS

If you have skin challenges on your face, like clogged pores due to oily skin referred to as blackheads, there is good news for you. Acne can be found on any part of your body, chest, neck, shoulders, or back. If you're a woman, sometimes it could be due to hormonal changes around that time of the month. If you are on a tight budget, this small list of inexpensive treatments will be very helpful to you. Some of these items you might already have in your cupboard or fridge. These things will help you dissolve the dead skin and oil that cause pimples and blackheads, and finally get rid of those unattractive eruptions. Remember to wash your face before using any of these recipes.

## Oatmeal Mask

Cook the oatmeal with distilled water. Let it cool and apply it to your face or any part of your body that has a blemish. Let it sit on the area for 15 – 20 minutes and rinse off with lukewarm water. Try this mixture once a day to say bye-bye to those pesky blemishes.

## Green Tea

Steep two bags of organic green tea in eight ounces of boiled water. Cool it until it is lukewarm, dab the mixture onto the blackheads. Let it dry on your face or wherever you have put it. Rinse with cool water, and dry before moisturizing your face. This is an easy daily routine to keep your skin free from any kind of blemishes, especially blackheads.

## Lemon Juice

Put one teaspoon of organic lemon juice into a bowl and dab any blackheads or blemishes you have. You can leave this on overnight, or use it once a day for ten minutes at a time. Use cool water to rinse it off. If you have picked at your skin, lemon juice can also prevent scarring.

## Epsom Salts Mask

Place four drops of iodine into a half-cup of warm water. Add one teaspoon of Epsom salts. Stir the mixture until the Epsom salts have dissolved. Make sure your hands are clean, and massage the mixture into your skin. After it is completely dry, wait a couple of minutes, and then wash it off with warm water, and dry. You can do this treatment as often as you like.

## Egg White Mask

I've saved this and the next for last because they do more than just dissolve the dead skin and oil that causes blackheads. These next two mixtures actually pull the dirt from the pores, and make for a quick removal of blackheads. Doing the next two treatments weekly could rid you of blackheads for the rest of your life.

There is a little pre-preparation for this one. Either lay out some toilet paper (enough to cover your face), or separate a two-ply tissue. Separate one egg white from the yolk. Apply a thin layer of egg white all over your face, place the toilet paper or tissue on top of the mixture. Press down lightly on the paper, and let it dry. When it is thoroughly dry, use your fingers to make a second layer right on top of the paper, then allow that to dry. When it has fully dried, peel it off your face, and rinse with cool to warm water, and moisturize.

# Baking Soda

Mix one tablespoon of baking soda with water to form a paste. Apply the paste to the problem areas, and let it dry for ten to fifteen minutes. Rinse with lukewarm water. If used regularly on spots or the entire face, this mixture will help get rid of oily skin which is the main cause of blackheads.

---

**TIP**
**Steam your face for at least five minutes, then use an ice cube to close the pores.**

---

**TIP**
**Always use a glass or ceramic bowl to make your mixtures.**

---

**TIP**
**Use a cotton ball or makeup pad when dabbing your face.**

---

**TIP**
**Be sure to exfoliate before your face treatment.**

---

**TIP**
**Always use warm water, not hot.**

> **TIP**
> Always pat your face dry. Never rub.

# FACE CREAMS and MAKEUP REMOVERS
## Moisturize

Your face is the first thing people see. It is also the most sensitive skin on your body. It is always taking on the sun, wind, rain, dust, and everything else that is out there. Moisturizing gives the skin on your face a barrier to protect you from these harmful elements. It also hydrates and gives you a more youthful glow. You can spend a lot of money on moisturizers. I know because I have. Then I discovered there are plenty of natural, inexpensive things you can use to hydrate your face as well as anything you'd find in a high-end salon. Here are a few of my discoveries.

> **TIP**
> Moisturize your face at least twice a day.

## Shea Butter

Another inexpensive way to keep your skin smooth and youthful is shea butter. I consider it a miracle product. I used shea butter on my stomach when I was pregnant with my kids, and after my stretched-out belly went back to normal, I never had one stretch mark. Shea butter is made from the nuts that are inside the fruit of the Shea tree, and is totally natural. Just massage it all over your body and you are good to go.

---

**TIP**
**It is important to check the expiration**
**date on your shea butter. If it has expired,**
**it has lost its moisturizing properties.**

---

# Coconut Oil

Coconut oil is my answer to almost everything. If you take one cup of coconut oil and two teaspoons of vitamin E oil and blend this mixture, for just pennies you will have enough moisturizer for at least six months or more.

# The Wonders of Coconut Oil

Coconut oil is good for:

- Psoriasis
- Eczema
- Oily skin
- Dry skin
- Redness
- Aging skin and wrinkles
- Scarring
- Sunburned or damaged skin
- Dry irritated lips
- Stretch marks
- Chemical-burned and radiated skin
- Dry, brittle, damaged hair

- Brittle nails and damaged cuticles
- Redness and inflammation associated with using Retin-A and glycolic acid

> **TIP**
> Melt the coconut oil in a double boiler, or in the oven on low heat. Never use a microwave. And always use extra virgin olive and coconut oil.

## Aloe Vera

I call aloe vera the miracle plant because I use it for so many things. Aloe is a succulent and has long pointy leaves. We have aloe growing in our yard, so it's easy for us to just walk outside and pick a leaf when we need to. My suggestion to you, if you live in an apartment or a place where it is hard to grow outside, just buy aloe in a flower pot and grow it inside. It's virtually indestructible and will grow anywhere there is no danger of freezing. To use it as a moisturizer, just cut off part of one of the leaves, slice the piece open, and use the gooey part inside on your face. When you are done, wrap the leftover stalk with cling wrap, and place it in the fridge. Next time you use it, the cooled aloe will feel even better on your face.

## Castor Oil

I developed an early prejudice against castor oil because it was used in a lot of old movies from the forties to treat kids who were getting or were already sick. Just a tablespoon would supposedly make them well, but the kids always made horrible faces at the thought of having to take it. Since those days, we've found other uses for castor oil.

Massaging just a few drops on your face before you go to sleep will keep your face from losing moisture and rejuvenate your skin.

## Vaseline

A lot of people think that Vaseline causes blemishes because it keeps the moisture from leaving your skin. Actually, it totally protects your skin from harsh winds and dryness while making your skin softer. People swimming long distances, mountain climbers, and others who have to protect their skin against extreme weather conditions will testify to its effectiveness. And it's a highly refined, triple-purified product that is regarded as a non-carcinogenic. What actually causes blemishes is not washing your face and removing all of your makeup, not Vaseline.

---

**TIP**
**Make sure you are using Vaseline
Petroleum Jelly and not a knock-off.**

---

## WHAT TO DO FOR OILY SKIN
## The Magic of Witch Hazel

There are so many good things I can say about witch hazel. I first learned about this miracle astringent when I was a kid in my mother's beauty salon. At that time, I thought witch hazel was a real witch with a long warty nose. I've since learned the truth. That was many years ago.

This skin care product is one of nature's oldest and best beauty secrets out there. Besides giving your face a smoother complexion, it's also soothing to the skin, and leaves your face with a beautiful glow.

Astringents are extremely effective cleaners and close the pores of your skin to help remove much of the oil. Alcohol-free witch hazel costs around $6.00 and lasts a long time.

---

**TIP**
**It is very important to always use alcohol-free witch hazel, and never use witch hazel that contains isopropyl alcohol.**

---

## Tightening Face and Neck Muscles.

To help build the muscles in your face and neck, I use the DermaWand or Suzanne Somers FaceMaster. The FaceMaster cost is over $200, but I've had mine for five years, and it's still going strong. You can get a DermaWand deal for about $100 online. After five years, that one is still going strong too. Even though this is a high cost item, it is a one-time buy. These devices stimulate the muscles under the skin by sending very low voltage currents from the wand to the face, thus toning the muscles. It's like a workout for your face.

You can use the wands while watching TV, or just before going to bed. Try to do it every night. If you skip a day or two, and you are doing everything else for your face and body, it really won't hurt your progress.

Your neck is another area that reveals the unwanted effects of aging.

Sometimes people just ignore the neck like it doesn't need any care at all. Wrong! Keep your neck clean and moisturized and use the wands as much as possible. There is another product that is the equivalent of working out with weights. It's called the Neckline Slimmer, and it's only $4.68 on Amazon.

However, if you don't want to spend any money, you can always do this simple neck exercise.

## Neck Tightening Exercise

Tilt your head back, tighten your neck, and open and close your mouth bringing your teeth together. Do this as you count to one hundred. This is another one with illustrations in Saba's *Autosize* section.

You can also use the wraps on your neck. (Wraps are explained in the skin section). The important thing is not to forget your neck. There's nothing that gives away your age like a beautifully smooth face on top of a wrinkly turkey neck.

## Teeth and Gums

Keeping your teeth white, and your gums healthy and firm, takes a little work. As you age, your teeth tend to yellow or take on an "off-white" color. This happens naturally, but it happens more quickly if you smoke, or drink a lot of tea or coffee. So, obviously, you would be doing yourself and your teeth and gums a favor by just quitting smoking. By now you have probably come to realize that smoking affects a lot more than just your teeth and gums. But that's another story.

I presume you want to keep your teeth, and if you are going to keep them, you might has well keep them white. It takes daily care. You've been told since you were a kid to brush after every meal. That's ideal, but not always practical for many people. Try to develop the habit of brushing after breakfast, before you start the rest of your day, and after dinner. And floss at least once a day. After dinner is a great time to floss, so you get rid of any leftovers before going to sleep. Personally, I had receding gums and needed surgery once. Never again. Now I try to floss after every meal and take care of my teeth and gums. My last checkup revealed perfect gums and teeth. Yay for me!

Maintaining healthy gums can be an ongoing battle. A product that really helped me is Oralive. It's used after you finish brushing your teeth. It kind of tastes like minty mud, but it's not as awful as it sounds, and has a ton of minerals and nutrients that really help your gums. Just swish it around your mouth for a minute or so with a little water. Then swallow it. The mud is really good for you and is full of nutrients that are good for your body, and the mint makes you forget you're swallowing mud.

The cost of Oralive is around $65, but it usually lasts about six or eight months. Sometimes even longer. You can order Oralive from www.ascendedhealth.com

If you can't afford or don't want to use mud in your mouth, check out my inexpensive whiten and heal alternative to Oralive below. But here are some other things you can try.

## Whitening Strip Alternative

If it's just whiteness you're looking for, I've found that Crest Whitestrips really work. That will run you $80 to $100 for a three or four-month supply. However, here is the alternative way to go if you can't afford those things.

Take a strip of cotton large enough to cover both your gums and your teeth, and dip it in hydrogen peroxide, which is available at almost any food or drugstore at under $3. Place it on the front side of your teeth for no longer than five minutes and go about your business. This method worked for me. You can repeat it only once a week, and it will bleach the white back into your teeth, while treating your gums. Try not to swallow any of it, but if you do it's not going to hurt you. Hydrogen peroxide will also help to clear up any infection you might have, and will help eliminate a lot of bad bacteria while it's whitening your teeth. This will only cost you around $3 for the year, or $1 if you go to the Dollar Store.

## Homemade Toothpaste

I am a big tea drinker, and tea tends to stain your teeth. When I drink iced tea, I always use a straw to bypass my teeth. I have tried everything I could to keep my teeth white and my gums healthy. After all the years of reading and listening to what everyone says on this subject, I decided to create my own toothpaste that is good for your gums, whitens your teeth, and tastes pretty good too. It's also cheaper than all the products out there. So give it a try if you like.

## Saba's Homemade Toothpaste

¼ cup of aluminum-free baking soda

¼ cup of sea salt

2 to 3 tablespoons of organic sulphur

A few drops of peppermint, spearmint, or vanilla to taste (get creative) 2 tablespoons of organic coconut oil – soft but not melted

Mix the baking soda, salt, and sulphur together. Then blend in the coconut oil. After all the ingredients are mixed well together, add the peppermint or your flavor of choice for taste. You now have enough personal health-filled toothpaste to last for a while. I keep about a week's worth of the mixture in the bathroom, and the rest in the fridge. Now go brush your teeth and smile.

---

**TIP**
**You can see me in action with**
**this recipe on my website.**

---

Here is that alternative recipe to Oralive that I told you about:

## Whiten and Heal Toothpaste

Hydrogen peroxide and baking soda also make a natural whitening toothpaste. You'll need:

¼ cup of hydrogen peroxide baking soda

Mix the baking soda in with the hydrogen peroxide until it has a pasty consistency and brush away germs and gum disease.

## Disclaimer:
**This worked great for me, but be sure and check with your dentist to make sure this will not hurt your crowns or dental implants.**

# CHAPTER 11:
# BE IT

Everything you've read about in this book is something I have done or used to get to my goal of being
a Bikini Diva/Sports Model. I don't use all of it anymore,
because I've reached my goal, and now I'm focused on
maintaining what I have. But I still use most of the tips
in this book, and I still use my affirmations and visualizations, and I meditate regularly. I also return to my
diets occasionally and continue to eat clean almost all
the time. It has become a lifestyle for me, and that is the
essence of Being It.

As I went through the process of becoming everything
I desired, I experienced a definite shift in consciousness.
I became more confident in everything I did because I
saw how I was bringing it about. I saw that I was responsible for changing my life. And most importantly, I had
a system that worked, not just for getting fit and looking
better, but for any goal I set for myself. I found the key to
unlocking the door to a greater, more fulfilling life.

In the past, I had always let obstacles and other people's opinions block me from attaining my desires. Once

I started living my Think It, Do It, Be It philosophy, life became more enjoyable. Every day became an adventure. I learned to say yes to things that I would have either resisted or accepted grudgingly before. And I found joy instead of doubts because I was changing the way I thought about things by repeating my affirmations and keeping a vivid visualization of exactly where I wanted to go ever present on my mind. I didn't have time for doubts because I was so focused on the creation of a new reality for myself. I learned to love a challenge, and now I feel like whatever I choose to do, I can accomplish it.

Most importantly, I learned to love myself in a healthy way, and accept everything about me and my body. Going through the Think It, Do It, Be It method, you can't help but learn to love yourself. It is a method that unlocks the limitations of the mind and refills your mind with "can do" inspiration. Once you realize that you are the one making the choices, and that you are the one acting on those choices, you can't help but love yourself for the effort and the gift of positive action.

My Think It, Do It, Be It, method works for me every day in big decisions or small ones. It's not only a part of my life, it's who I have become. I have turned my body into a youthful looking body. My face, although it has a few wrinkles, also has a youthful glow to it. Now I am going to use my Think It, Do It, Be It, method to clean out my garage and my closets, so I can move through the rest of my life free of things I no longer need, while making room for new things that feed me positive energy. Now I want to move to Hawaii with ease in the next couple of years. To that I say, "and so it is."

# The Ride of Life

Living a life of knowing is an amazing thing. Being in show business all my life has proven to be quite challenging. There are ups and downs and twists and turns with every project I have taken on. Before I discovered my method, I never knew what to expect from day to day, and what was going on would usually take me for a ride of its own. I was often a victim of life. I would, more often than I'd like to admit, succumb to depression, sickness, and fear. The minute things didn't go the way I thought they should, I would doubt myself and the things I was doing. It was easier for me to just get sick over things so I could hide away with my fear of failure. Being in show business as an actor, writer, producer, and director gave me lots of avenues to fail. Before I started practicing my method, anything that didn't work for me would make me feel like a failure. As a mother, if anything would go wrong with one of my kids, it was, of course, all my fault. I'm sure some things were, but even after I woke up and saw things more clearly, I still carried some of that blame, shame and regret along for the ride.

Becoming a Bikini Diva through the Think It, Do It, Be It method was the best thing that ever happened to me. It proved to me that what I was thinking could become a reality if I gave it my time and focus. I still payed attention to my husband, family, and business. After all, they were part of the life I wanted for myself, but what I had to do to become a Bikini Diva became my number one driving force. I kept to my vision of what I wanted. I affirmed constantly, both quietly to myself and out loud. I carried pictures with me of what I visualized I would look like when I reached my goal. Every time I opened the fridge and saw that little picture of a professional Bikini Diva that I taped up in there to remind me, I thought, "Some day…". Even when I messed up on a meal or workout, I knew that I was still dedicated to my goal and would succeed. I didn't beat myself up about it. I was kind to myself and affirmed that messing up now and then would not stop me from reaching my goal. It was like, if you fall off a horse, pick yourself up and get back on.

Every day, through every affirmation, I was slowly strengthening my mind-muscle. I was changing my belief system and changing my entire lifestyle. I became aware of life as a process. Moment by moment, I was doing what had to be done to reach my goal. It wasn't until two years into living the method, that I opened the fridge and there I was! I was seventy years old, and my body looked like that picture in the fridge.

I started applying the method to other areas of my life, and soon found that I was not being affected by minor setbacks in business or at home. I started focusing on each moment, and always kept the end result clearly in my sights. I was always a happy person in public, but now I was a happy person when I was alone. My method (the shift) didn't happen overnight, but it happened.

## Expansion of Love

I learned to believe in myself. The more I found that I could trust myself to follow through and live up to the promises I had made to myself, the more I learned to love myself. And the more I loved myself, the more I found love to give to others. I found a wellspring of love that is inexhaustible. I found an abundance of love for my husband, my family, my friends, and even complete strangers. I am a hugger. The act of hugging is my constant reminder to myself of how much love I have to give, and how it is never limited to just a few. Everyone deserves a hug.

I was finally able to live a fearless life knowing that whatever was happening was for my highest and best good. I knew that whatever was going on in the world, I was able to take care of myself. I no longer judged things as good or bad. They just were what they were, and it was only my reaction to them that made them positive or negative. The love I have learned to have for myself has spilled over into all of life. I love everyone in my life so much more fully, and I experience the fullness that comes from knowing, as the Beatles wrote, "…love is all there is."

## Meditation and Contacting the Power

My practice of meditation started with a commitment. When I was a kid, I committed to becoming a dancer. I didn't start out as a dancer. It took many years of practice. First, I had to learn the steps. Then I had to learn how to put those steps together. After a while, I was dancing with ease. With meditation, I went through a similar process. First, I learned to quiet my mind so I could actually get in touch with the power within. We all have that power. It just takes practice to learn how to sit quietly and allow the recognition of that power to become part of your consciousness. You'll know when you've contacted that power because it becomes a transformative event. You feel the connection to it. It is always available, and you can tap into it, and use it to reach any goal you have set forth for yourself.

And it all started by sitting quietly in meditation and inviting it into my life. It is the same power and energy that flows in and through all things. It's like plugging an electric cord into a socket, and all of a sudden there is light. Meditation is the cord that connects me to the power. Once I relax enough to allow that connection, I can affirm my most intimate desires, either out loud or to myself, and know that life's energy will start working to produce those desires for me. I visualize it being done. I fill myself with joy, knowing that it is done, and watch as life rises to meet me on my terms. I end my meditation with the words, "And so it is," and I believe it. The process has begun, and I'm along for the ride. I do everything I can to live "as if" everything is working for me, and still allow this perfect life force to deliver it to me as it sees fit. I make no demands on how it will happen. I simply live knowing it will. I don't let little successes and failures distract me along the way. I can't worry about every bump in the road, but I know that as long as I take this road, I'm heading toward my goals and that the end result is inevitable.

You can reach any goal you desire by believing and knowing what the outcome will be. You can let the energy of knowing work for you. Some people freak out over hearing the word "praying." I understand that. If you don't want to call it praying, call it connecting to your energy source. That is what I do. I plug into my energy source and allow it to take me to my desired goal, and you can do that too. See it, believe it, be it.

This book focuses on your goals in creating a new body for yourself, because that's where I started the process myself. But you don't have to stop there. You can make your goal about anything in your life. Just know the first step is to think it. If you think you want to do something, then do it by making a list of everything you need to do to reach that goal.

Visualize and affirm it every day. Believe it and do it. Know that if you do it, you can manifest it. I love my life, and my greatest joy would be to see that you all learn to love yours as much. Remember the secret formula:

Think It, Do It, Be It.

# LISTS

## HEALTHY SHOPPING LIST
### Proteins
Beef

Chicken – breast or thigh (skinless) Crabmeat – frozen is okay

Eggs

Fish – any white fish

Shrimp – frozen from Costco or Smart & Final Wild or wild caught salmon only

### Vegetarian/ Vegan Proteins
Black beans

Edamame (soybeans in a pod) Lentils

Nuts – almonds, Brazil nuts, pecans, pistachios, walnuts, macadamia Seeds – pumpkin, hemp, chia, sunflower, sesame

Tofu

**Grains** Barley Brown rice Bulger Faro

Oats, Oatmeal Quinoa

Spelt Wild rice

**Vegetables** Asparagus Avocado Beans, string Beets
    Broccoli
Brussel sprouts Cabbage Carrots Cauliflower
Celery Cilantro Cucumbers Lettuce Onions Parsley
Peas, sugar snap
Peppers – green, red, yellow, orange Spinach
Tomatoes/cherry tomatoes
Potatoes – yams and sweet Kale and kale salad

**Fruit** Apples Avocados
Berries – blueberries, strawberries, raspberries
Kiwis
Pears Pomegranates

**Tropical and Sugary Fruits (eat sparingly)**
Bananas Papayas Watermelon

**Snacks**
Almond butter/peanut butter (natural/unsweetened)
Crackers – brown rice, Mary's, pecan crackers (limit to
    under 10) Chips – veggie and flaxseed tortilla chips
    (limit to under 10) Hummus
Nuts – almonds, Brazil nuts, pecans, pistachios, walnuts,
    macadamia Seeds – pumpkin, sunflower, squash

**Seasonings and Things for Cooking**
Avocado oil Butter
Coconut oil – extra virgin
Salt – Himalayan pink, kosher salt, or sea salt Flour –
    almond, coconut or quinoa

Olive oil – extra virgin Seaweed sheets
Sweeteners – stevia, agave, honey

## Bread
Dave's Killer Bread
Ezekiel sprouted grain tortillas
Whole grain and seeded bread with no additives

## Drinks
Tea – green, mint, any herbal
Almond milk, coconut milk, or soy milk

## Canned and Packaged Things
Protein powder-Choose low sugar brands and non-dairy
    if possible Pink salmon-wild, in water
Tuna fish-wild, in water
Organic Jack's Cantina Style Salsa Trader Joe's Cuban
    Style Black Beans

# Essentials for the Think it, Do it, Be it! Diet

**Good things to have:**
A cooler Ice packs
Stainless steel water bottle Ziplock bags
Tight sealed containers

**Breakfast**
Oatmeal – apple – berries

**Protein Drink**
Protein powder – almond milk – blueberries – banana
    – nuts

**Veggie Drink (any or all of these ingredients)**
Green leafy vegetable or herbs: kale, spinach, mustard
    greens, collard greens, cabbage, cilantro, parsley, etc.
Peppers (red or green), broccoli, green beans, celery,
    ginger, or any veggie
Berries: blueberries, strawberries, raspberries
Avocado or banana for thickening

## Morning Snack
Pumpkin, sunflower or squash seeds – unsalted Peanuts
   or pistachio nuts in the shell – unsalted
Walnuts or almonds
Carrots and hummus
Celery and almond butter or peanut butter (natural,
   without sugar or additives)

**Lunch** Salad Wrap

**If you're making your own lunch**
Dave's Killer Bread
Ezekiel sprouted grain tortilla Hard-boiled egg
Shrimp or crabmeat Cucumber
Avocado
Sweet snap peas Tomatoes

**Afternoon Snack**
Same as morning snack or choose:
Zone Bar
Think Thin Bar Saba's mock candy

## Dinner
Chicken, beef, or fish Green vegetable Sweet potato or
   yam Salad
Oil & vinegar dressing
Green tea

# Daily Checklist

A good habit takes at least twenty-one days to develop. If you need more, just copy these and create more days.

## Week One

☐☐☐☐☐☐☐ I did my morning gratitude session
☐☐☐☐☐☐☐ I set my mood for my day
☐☐☐☐☐☐☐ Incorporated all of the exercises into my daily routine
☐☐☐☐☐☐☐ Incorporated some of the exercises into my daily routine
☐☐☐☐☐☐☐ I have practiced my fire breath
☐☐☐☐☐☐☐ I had no sugar today
☐☐☐☐☐☐☐ I have limited my sugar intake
☐☐☐☐☐☐☐ I followed the healthy food suggestions completely
☐☐☐☐☐☐☐ I ate smaller portions than usual

## Week Two

☐☐☐☐☐☐☐ I did my morning gratitude session
☐☐☐☐☐☐☐ I set my mood for my day

☐☐☐☐☐☐☐ Incorporated all of the exercises into my daily routine

☐☐☐☐☐☐☐ Incorporated some of the exercises into my daily routine

☐☐☐☐☐☐☐ I have practiced my fire breath

☐☐☐☐☐☐☐ I had no sugar today

☐☐☐☐☐☐☐ I have limited my sugar intake

☐☐☐☐☐☐☐ I followed the healthy food suggestions completely

☐☐☐☐☐☐☐ I ate smaller portions than usual

## Week Three

☐☐☐☐☐☐☐ I did my morning gratitude session

☐☐☐☐☐☐☐ I set my mood for my day

☐☐☐☐☐☐☐ Incorporated all of the exercises into my daily routine

☐☐☐☐☐☐☐ Incorporated some of the exercises into my daily routine

☐☐☐☐☐☐☐ I have practiced my fire breath

☐☐☐☐☐☐☐ I had no sugar today

☐☐☐☐☐☐☐ I have limited my sugar intake

☐☐☐☐☐☐☐ I followed the healthy food suggestions completely

☐☐☐☐☐☐☐ I ate smaller portions than usual

# Nine-Day Diet Food List

Asparagus Avocado

Black beans (canned or dried) Celery

Cherry tomatoes Coconut oil Eggs (3 dozen)

Hummus (choose your flavors) Lentils (for soup)

Salmon, wild caught (frozen or fresh) Spinach

String beans

Sweet peas/sugar snap peas (fresh) Yams or sweet
   potatoes

# Products

**Shampoos**

Ovation – For damaged hair

Pantene Pro – V Nature Fusion Smooth Vitality – For dry or brittle hair

Garnier Fructis – For curly or wavy hair

Herbal Essence – Makes fine hair look thicker Vive Pro by L'Oreal – Perks up your highlights

**Conditioners**

Pantene – For regular hair

Frizz Ease – For frizzy or treated hair Tresemme – Regular hair

Infusium – Regular hair

Herbal Essence – Regular hair

**Treatments**

Jojoba oil

Rosemary essential oil Avocado

Pomegranate seed oil

Coconut oil

Maruga oil Argan oil

**Moisturizer** Coconut oil Vitamin E oil Aloe vera Castor oil
Vaseline Petroleum Jelly Witch hazel – alcohol free
Eucerin Daily Protection moisturizer Murad Essential C
Cucumber peel

**Masks** Oatmeal Green tea Lemon juice Egg whites
Baking soda Honey
Banana, raw honey, lemon juice Papaya, raw honey,
    lemon juice Avocados

**Face & Neck**
DermaWand
Suzanne Somers FaceMaster

**Teeth & Gums** Hydrogen peroxide Oralive
Aluminum-free baking soda Sea salt
Organic sulphur
Peppermint, vanilla, or any flavoring
Organic coconut oil

**Body**
Scrub – coffee grounds, sugar, salt, coconut oil or extra
    virgin olive oil
Shea butter
Coconut oil
Aloe vera – in a tube or buy a plant
Epsom salts

**Wrap**

The Wrap – by It Works

Can be ordered through www.ThinkitDoitBeit.us

**Red Light Therapy**

Look for it in a location near you.

# AFFIRMATIONS

### Affirmations to start the Think It, Do It, Be It program

*I am excited about taking action toward being fit.*

*I can do this program one day at a time.*

*I am in control of my choices.*

*I make healthy choices for myself.*

*Today I will drop all judgment of myself and others. I am grateful for this wonderful day.*

*I deserve to be happy and healthy.*

### Affirmations for Meditation

*I see myself getting healthier and more fit every day. I accept change with ease.*

*Whatever I envision, I can do.*

### Affirmations for Meal Prepping

*I have plenty of time for my new diet and for my new lifestyle.*

*I know the choices I am making now are the reason I will reach my goal!*

### Affirmations for Using Smaller Plates

*My stomach is completely satisfied with this meal.*

*The amount of food I'm eating nourishes me completely.*

## Affirmations for Switching to Sugar-Free Things
*This candy is delicious and satisfying.*
*I am eating chocolate and still losing weight.*
*This chocolate candy is good for me, and I can have a couple of pieces guilt free.*
*I am happy to be changing the way I eat sweets.*
*This is a great way to be satisfied as I cut sugar out of my diet.*

## Affirmations for Peaking Your Family and Friends' Interest
*I know everyone can see the difference in my body and attitude. What I am doing for myself has a good effect on others around me.*
*As I get healthier, thinner, and stronger, it is easier to share my experience.*
*Through my choices, I am becoming an inspiration to others.*

## Affirmations for A DAY IN THE LIFE OF THINK IT, DO IT, BE IT
### Morning
*I am grateful that I stretch with ease as I get closer to my goal.*

### Morning Break Time
*I am doing everything necessary for a healthier and stronger body. I love how I feel, and I love how I look.*

### Before Lunch
*I am excited about taking action toward being fit.*

### Lunch Time
*This choice is helping me reach my goal with ease.*

*My craving for unhealthy things is diminishing. I am grateful for that.*

## After Lunch

*I am satisfied with what I'm feeding my body. I am rewarded by feeling healthy and fit.*
*Every day it gets easier and easier.*

## Affirmations for Dinner

*Thank you for this healthy food. I know that it is helping me to create the healthy body I desire.*

## Affirmations for Before Sleep

*It gets easier for me to do healthy things for myself day after day.*
*I love my body, and I love how the changes I've made in body and mind are working for me.*

## Affirmations for THE NINE-DAY DIET

*Calories don't count when I am eating sensibly.*
*With all healthy food, I know I am getting thinner with each meal I eat. Eating this way becomes easier for me every day.*
*Thank you for this healthy food. I know that it is helping me to create the healthy body I desire.*

## Affirmations & Visualizations for AUTOSIZE
## Stretching Visualization

*Visualize your muscles relaxing and lengthening.*

## Affirmation

*I let my body relax as I let go of stress and tension.*

## Chest Visualization

*Visualize the chest you would like to have. See a well-shaped chest lifting and getting firmer and stronger with every pulse or hold.*

## Affirmation

*As I strengthen my chest, I strengthen my resolve.*

## Arms Visualization

*Visualize a sleek, tight, shapely arm. (The way it used to be or the way you desire it to be.)*

## Affirmation

*My arms are tight and shapely.*

## Abs Visualization

*Visualize yourself with a tight, flat stomach.*

## Affirmation

*I feel my power as I strengthen my core.*

## Thighs and Glutes Visualization

*Visualize your thighs getting tighter and firmer and your glutes getting rounder and tighter.*

## Affirmation

*I am developing magnificent glutes and thighs.*

## Legs Visualization

*Visualize stronger, shapelier legs.*

## Affirmation
*As I shape and strengthen my legs, I move forward with ease.*

## Neck Visualization
*Visualize a smooth and elegant neck.*

## Affirmation
*My head sits atop a strong and elegant neck.*

## Fingers, Wrists, and Hands Visualization
*Visualize your fingers and hands looking smooth and youthful.*

## Affirmation
*My hands and wrists are smooth and flexible.*
And…I can now open jars easier!

## Affirmations for YOUTHFUL BODY AND SKIN
## Hair
*What I am doing for my hair is bringing back the youthful look.*
*My hair is getting healthier with every stroke.*

## Face
*My face radiates the health and beauty within.*

www.ingramcontent.com/pod-product-compliance
Lightning Source LLC
Chambersburg PA
CBHW071945090426
42740CB00011B/1832